Mike Hayward, ready for action, Lachung Chu, Sikkim

Having paddled more than 300 rivers in 23 countries over 40 years Mike Hayward has a habit of seeking out new challenges. He is a keen outdoor adventurer who still explores by river and sea kayak, canoe and mountain bike. Not deterred by standing out from the crowd, he previously published 'Rivers of Cumbria' and then widened his horizons, in a series of seemingly more challenging adventures. He has led expeditions around the globe including unpaddled rivers in UK, Nepal and Sikkim. Mike is still an active paddler, utilising his extensive knowledge, sharing new adventures and inspiring fellow paddlers with his enthusiasm.

To my paddling friends who have been enthusiastic enough, again and again, to share our adventures on so many river trips. I could not have done it without you.

Sten Sture, Chris Walker, Richard Evans, Robin Everingham, Gareth Walker and too many others to name.

Mike Hayward

JUST AROUND THE NEXT CORNER

Adventures with kayaks

AUSTIN MACAULEY PUBLISHERS™

LONDON • CAMBRIDGE • NEW YORK • SHARJAH

A CIP catalogue record for this title is available from the British Library.

ISBN 9781035824038 (Paperback)
ISBN 9781035824045 (ePub e-book)

www.austinmacauley.com

First Published 2022
Austin Macauley Publishers Ltd®
1 Canada Square
Canary Wharf
London
E14 5AA

20230109

I would like to acknowledge the following people for their contributions:

Chris Walker for allowing me to use his diary notes and most of the pictures of myself. Especially in Corsica, Costa Rica and Scotland.

George Novak for sharing his Sikkim photos. Rachel Powell for the photos of myself on the Cree. Sten Sture for photos in Scotland and Sikkim.

Andy Hall for his photo of me in the 'Green wall' Bio Bio, Brian Clough for his photos of me on the Vagastie and Einig, the stranger who sent me his photos of Skelwith force.

Pete Knowles, 'Slime' for supplying advice and a map of Coruh. Raphael Gallo for helping sort the Costa Rica trip.
Eric Leaper for leading us around Chile.

Dick McCullum and his raft team for guiding us down the Grand Canyon trip and facilitating our timescale by splitting the journey.

Ajeet Bajaj, for dealing with all the administration, relating to our exploration of Sikkim.

The Sikkim Tourist board for so generously supporting our trip to Sikkim. To Malden Mills, the USA, for providing us with our Purple Polartec tops in Sikkim. All the guidebook writers who helped by sharing their insights into where to paddle.

Friends who joined me on various trips in the UK, the Alps and further afield, providing safety cover and encouraging my enthusiasm.

Andrew 'Loz', Lawrence for seeing and imagining a Scrimbly.
Google Earth for the image of the upper Tarn gorge.
Shutterstock for the image of the Hoopoe Bird.

Table of Contents

Chris Cartwright, popping out on Boite, Italy

Pushing My Limits

Skelwith Force,
River Brathay (September 1985)

I had been paddling on and off for a few years when I moved to the Lake District. The local paddling community was a little reluctant, since a local paddler, Ron Treptoe had been pinned in his kayak for a couple of hours on Pillar falls, Great Langdale Beck. He was only able to breathe from a pocket of air, which formed as water flowed around and over his head. The mountain rescue team used ropes and a ladder to free him. After Ron's episode, there was a mood of pessimism amongst the local paddlers. While they were not without good skills, there seemed little enthusiasm to seek new horizons or in some cases, even paddle at all.

Undeterred, I found a few willing mates up for a challenge and adventure. The next time it rained hard, as we descended the same Great Langdale Beck, the class 4 Pillar falls rapid seemed to grow in stature, but inspection allowed us to consider the 'line'. It went, no problem. Our elation was short-lived, we paddled across Elterwater when talk of Skelwith falls came to the fore. We recounted tales of a scoutmaster who had died trying to paddle the falls and another of a fisherman washed over in a rowing boat, who also met the same fate. So, when we arrived at the portage I decided to have a look at the 5 m drop.

Not too bad I thought.

The water level was high but offered a tongue of green water, on the middle left, which did not exist at lower levels. Just above this, a stopper wave might be a problem, but with enough speed…

So I carried my boat back above the falls and prepared to launch. Funny how the brain works – as I pushed off a line from the Star Wars film (all the rage at the time) came into my head – 'may the force be with you!'

Fortunately, it was.

The author paddles Skelwith Force

This photo was taken by an onlooker, a little out of focus. But at least it is a record of the event. Maybe it was a first descent?

Note the Dancer – a pointy-nosed kayak, Ace helmet, and flat Ottersport paddles. Local paddlers fall over these falls for fun nowadays. How things change.

River grades

Grade	Description	Reality	Actuality
1	Gentle flow. Some small waves.	Float down with no problems.	You'll need to make an effort to go.
2	Faster flowing water. Some rocks to avoid. Large-eddy pools. Some larger waves.	Choice of routes. Routes are easy to follow.	At least I don't have to paddle much! Starting to move and steer.
3	Faster water with larger waves small stoppers. Smaller or tighter eddies.	Full control of your kayak needed. Move kayak with more accuracy. Route easily seen and followed.	Interesting.
4	More continuous rapids and waves. Some stoppers hold boats. Eddies fewer and smaller. Narrow gorges some risk of entrapment on obstructions.	Route not always easily distinguished. Precise control with fast accurate decisions needed. Difficulty in picking out features of chosen route when on water.	Naughty but nice.
5	As 4 but taken to extreme continuous large and/or irregular falls and rapids.	Difficult to choose a route and follow the line. Sometimes impossible to follow your line on the water, due to ever-changing water features. Waves may break over your head.	Oh my! Will I make it? I'll be pleased when it's done.
6	Wild and unpredictable water, high falls with deep pools.	Go with the flow but try to pre-empt it Total submergence entirely possible. Chosen route difficult to attain.	Paddle with instinct. Foaming white death.
X	Extremely high falls, blocked rocky rapids, sumps.	Not paddleable	Portage

Tentative Steps

First Visit to the Alps (May 86)

Chris Dale, Paul Doolan

Those who have been there will know that the Inn in Austria is rather a large volume river. This was rather a surprise to us since two weeks previously, we had been on the river Mint near Kendal, 10 m wide at best, low water, scraping the rocks just to get down. The Inn is one of the Alps' biggies, almost 70 m across and flowing fast with so much water that the Mint wouldn't be noticed if it ran alongside. The old broken weir below Tosens boasts 3 m high waves during the spring flood. Chris Dale and I looked at each other and wondered if we should be here. But of course, that is why we were here -to test ourselves. Although very powerful, Paul, Chris and I found no real problems negotiating the waves, though I don't recall having much idea of what to do except to keep paddling and avoid the big holes. Doing the wiggle dance, and trying to keep at right angles to the breaking waves seemed to work effectively.

Chris on the Trisanna – note the fibreglass 'Everest' boat

As the week went by, our confidence grew, taking in the easier grade 3 upper sections of the Trisanna, Pitzbach and Sill and the more powerful 'wood yard' section of the Inn to Landeck.

Of course, we were buoyant with our success so we decided to try on the grade 4 Sanna. About 2 km from the put-in, but only a few minutes on the river to the infamous Wolfsculcht, class 4/5. The Wolfsculcht is the sort of rapid in which adrenaline starts to flow, so your stomach becomes involved, and thoughts like 'what if!' begin to roll around your grey matter and have to be banished from your mind. If you can put the thoughts aside and be rational you can plan a way past the holes, thus avoiding the upwelling on the inside corner. The big hole on the right seemed best avoided, but the left was tricky too – still we could do it – and we did, running the left hole directly – no problem, we were buzzing. For a few km further on, the river is flatter, only class 3, but a bit swirly and then turns right and heads off down the class 4 'graveyard' at Pianz.

The graveyard is so-called due to a 500 m long section of boulders looking like headstones, steeper chutes between them and many holding stoppers. This is paddle it on sight territory, with no real backup except those you paddle with.

Unfortunately, Paul needed his fellow paddlers. Two-thirds of the way down, he angled into a stopper, and capsized and by the time Chris and I got to him he had failed to roll; come out of his boat; been rolled and bashed against numerous rocks and boulders. With Chris's help, Paul managed to clamber onto the back of my kayak and I paddled him to the right bank. Paul seemed OK at first. But of course, he was not. Chris and I, a throw line, four German paddlers, in three hours, saw us leaving Paul in the hospital with a concussion, severe bruising and a copy of his insurance document to read.

The next morning saw Chris and I on the ever so big and bouncy Imst section of the Inn, rescuing a German chap's boat about 1 km after he swam.

The following day saw us on a class 4 section of the upper Rosanna, only 1500 m long. Planning out the route seemed to be the best strategy at each stage so we walked along the banks, as safety was in our minds!

It took all afternoon to run this section. (Some years later, we ran the same section in a few minutes without inspection).

The author on the Rosanna

A few days later, Paul came out of the hospital and we moved north to the Lech valley where it snowed. Fortunately, Rudi's campsite had a hut where we could cook, chill out and meet some more German paddlers. The Elephants Teeth section of the Lech was recommended; and though quite long, it proved to be relatively easy.

The same evening, our new German friends dragged us along to a meeting of local paddlers, the aim to 'save the Lech gorges'. We had never heard of the Lech Gorges and had no idea why they needed saving, even after all the speeches. But then it all became clear, there were plans to construct several dams in the gorges.

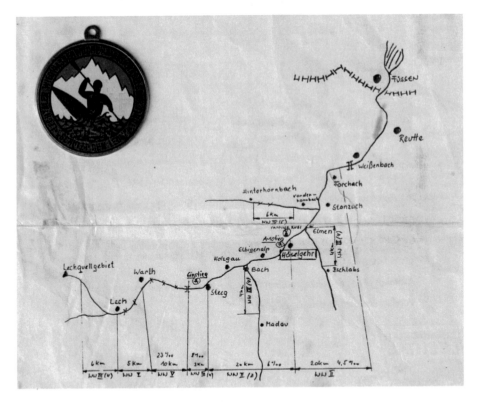

Lech river map

We were shown an 8mm cine film of some 'nutters' in very long fibreglass kayaks falling down a very long sequence of waterfalls. Well, that was it, I had to do them. The Lech gorge became my target, but first I would need to gain a few more skills.

We were even awarded a medal for supporting the event.

Why Paddle at All?

Why do I kayak wild rivers when clearly there are easier alternatives? There are many answers to this simple question.

Most start kayaking for a laugh, and a bit of fun with their mates. Once you have managed to grasp the basics of how to control your kayak, then you might seek out places to try out your skills: surf ever bigger waves, cross expanses of ocean, or journey along the coast. Perhaps try more rocky rivers for higher falls. Whichever, the challenge is both intellectual, emotional and physical. On a white water river, I liken it to seeking the route through a three-dimensional maze. With confidence, you can 'succeed safely. Working out the route from the boat and paddling it successfully without inspection, is much more satisfying than with prior inspection, even if it requires more bottle to do so.

Others would quote the 'being there' or 'the journey' syndrome, the situation, the views, the scenery, and the weird rock sculpture. Perhaps it is getting to places, never or not easily visited by foot, or through a deep gorge or the thick rain forest. Floating through a remote place; admiring those huge limestone towers; venturing into weird environments; seal launching below overhanging cliffs; where arches and smoothed rock amphitheatres abound. These sentiments are enhanced when you venture into a gorge, like the Upper Hinter Rhine, vertical-sided, and imposing, where thoughts of 'has anyone been here?' prevail, even though you know, usually, that many have been there before. There is the awe of looking up from the bottom of a 700 m deep gorge like the Verdon where the sides are only 5 m apart, thinking 'wonder if I could climb out if I have to?'. The simple awareness of how small and insignificant and unimportant you really are. The sense that when you turn that bend, the challenge is always a new one. You wonder if you will be able to deal with the water level, the water features, the rocks, tree hazards or a combination of these. There is only one way to find what is around the next corner.

There is the exploration factor, when you seek out those rivers that have rarely, or never, been paddled before. Increasingly more difficult to find, but for the ardent map searcher or worldly explorer, they do still exist. When you do find such a gem, every paddle stroke seems to put you in the phase of pushing the limits and exploring the frontier, irrespective of grade. Though the experience is enhanced by more difficult water. It is evident that when paddling 'new' water in a group there is always an unstated 'race' to get to and paddle that new fall or rapid first. Until, of course, you suddenly consider your well-being and the situation and adopt a more wimpish mode of hiding in micro eddies and smiling, as someone else is forced into the front, to be a probe, even though they thought they were following you.

There is that aspect when you simply get scared and the pleasure is only gleaned after you have escaped and survived, to complete the adventure. You live on the adrenaline rush. These are the times when, if you are lucky, the group's emotional bonding comes to the fore, with a laugh, despite the potential seriousness of the situations you have been in. But you can be unlucky; even when you are confident, the inevitable can happen. Perhaps a capsize, a pin on a rock, floating under a branch or getting pushed off course so that you have to run the route that you had dismissed, as not desirable. Your skills, experience and all that practice kick in, combined with your self-confidence, and arrogance -it won't happen to me. You cope and become more aware of yourself and as a result, put it down to building your expertise.

Then there is the line where adventure becomes misadventure. The closer to the line, the better the adventure, but there are those times when you cross the line. You push the limit too far or you simply misjudge your ability or the water. It doesn't matter, the consequence is the same; it all goes wrong so you are simply out of control. It can be terminal. But usually, through luck and more luck the outcome is still good, you survive and question your existence and why you did it. You consider, will I come back for more? Yes, of course, you will, more is essential because this is your reason for being, and because if you didn't come back for more, you wouldn't get into a similar position in the first place – you wouldn't get near that line of misadventure.

Some do it for sheer pleasure: surfing that wave or playing that hole. Gleaning pleasure through the expression of your skill, you get stuck in and show off your crazy stunts. These are the posers, the playboys. But when it comes to the crunch in a real situation, do they cope? The best do, the less able just survive.

Less talented freeze and go home, so confident in their ability, but so unaware of the situation, they misjudge their limitations. It can be dangerous, however careful management of the risk, will reduce the chance of a negative outcome The real truth is that it is **simply fun**; the combination of, skill, challenge, the environment, the journey, and exploration, near the limit of your adventure and the pleasure. It is rare to experience them all, but occasionally on one trip…it all comes together.

Acronyms

FWD	Foaming white death
ITS	Intention to Swim
LES	Last eddy syndrome
PFE	Potential for epic
DIB	Doing it bit
Aero	Feeling bubbles all around you
FLW	Funny little wave
PI	Precautionary Ibuprofen
MOT	Moment of trepidation
OTI	Open to Interpretation
LOST	Lack of strategic thinking

Having just entered a klamm in which there was PFE. I was glad to have had my PI to ease yesterday's aches. We had already arrived at the DIB. As I was leading the last section, LES kicked in just above the next drop. The way on was OTI, no place for LOST though. The right was FWD, whereas on the left I could see an FLW. Left it was, an MOT as I approached the drop, then fall, aero and smiles.

The author shoots the main falls – Vagastie

Upupa epops

Easter 1988 Upper Allier, the last river on my first 10-day trip in the Central Massif of France. We spent some time in the Ardeche Region and Tarn gorges, paddling a variety of rivers. The long but very easy Ardeche limestone canyon; steep granite slabs of the Lot and Tarn. The easier but flooded Tarnon and the narrow boulder-filled limestone gorge of the Jonte amongst others.

Towards the end, we took a chance and drove north to the Allier, camping at Chaperoux. Fortune favoured us since the Allier was on the dam release, so oodles of water flowed through the remote countryside. With all the stress of the harder rivers were behind us We were paddling fit and a well-honed team. The Upper Allier proved the perfect final trip, with clear water, warm sun, with fine rapids, being most tricky at the end. Life felt good.

During the shuttle for the upper Allier, we spotted a Hoopoe bird, *Upupa epops*. This was not something anyone had seen before – something of a rarity. Though an argument ensued as to whether it was a Jay. We laughed for ages. On our paddling trips for years later, we supposedly saw many hoopoes, without actually seeing any. It became a standing joke.

Somehow that one moment seemed to capture the mood of our adventure. We resolved to return for more adventures and find more hoopoes. It is so strange how these moments grab us and capture our imagination.

Spotting the rare hoopoe was akin to paddling all the new rivers we had just discovered for the first time. The hoopoe becomes my guide, perhaps.

Funnily enough, despite keeping an eye out over the years, many possible sightings remained unconfirmed. We did not see another hoopoe until…

As I recount these tales, some of which, on reflection seem ever so scary. It seems for some strange reason, these incidents, the near misses, disproportionately stick in the mind and yield the strongest memories. Some are recounted in this book. In truth, the vast majority of kilometres of the rivers pass without incident. Usually, many days on the river pass with only fun and pleasure derived. I suppose it's when you are closer to that line of misadventure when your skills and experience are tested, that your strongest images become imprinted. Capsizes are not common. However, they do occur because the paddler is caught out, and so can be an indication of how tricky the paddling is. Capsizes can be rectified with a roll, or a swim ensues.

White water paddling is essentially safe. Scary moments are infrequent and bad times are as rare as spotting a hoopoe, but stray too far…

Rescue

River Orchy (December 1985)

Gareth Walker, Wayne Brunton and I arrived at the Bridge of Orchy hotel. The landlord informed us the Orchy was in its biggest flood for two years, PFE to be sure. The river flowed almost level with the minor road that ran beside it. The deep chasm of forestry falls was washed out, now just some large standing waves. Our choice, is to paddle, go elsewhere or not at all.

Anything but the first option would have been a wise decision. However, the combination of naivety and enthusiasm won through. We decided to paddle.

We found an ingress just above the bridge by the hotel. The fact we had a swim to deal with on the first rapid, should have made us question our decision.

Onwards. Tested by large bouncy waves where Scrimblies loomed. In less than 2 km the inevitable became a reality. Wayne was thrown over by a large wave train. He didn't roll and swam through some lovely large holes. I managed to clip his kayak with my towline before assisting his swim to the bank. Wayne lay there, half in the river, coughing up river water. I was hanging on to a small tree branch, being pulled under by an overfull kayak still attached to me by my towline. Since I was using both hands to cling to the tree branch I was unable to reach for my quick-release buckle. I shouted to him for help. Then I cursed him, but he was unable to respond. My strength waned, so my grip slipped. Eventually, the river's pull overcame my resolve, dragging me under some low branches. I had to bail out, the scrambled up the soggy, muddy bank Wayne's kayak in tow. However, my boat and paddle set off to do a solo descent of the river. Wayne soon recovered, but my pride and my bringer of happiness was gone. The following day, we spotted my kayak in a field some 50m from the river 9km downstream, now only at a high level. It had navigated the whole river, including the narrow slot of Forestry Falls, submerged under the deluge. I resolved not to use my towline unless it was absolutely safe to do so.

Yugoslavia (July 1987)

We had been paddling in the now-divided Yugoslavia and discovered the literally white waters of the Soca, caused by eroded glacial rock flour suspended in the flow. There we met a group of German paddlers and being open to suggestions, we travelled two days south to meet them at the Tara. The offer of class 3, such clear water, combined with a two-day trip through a deep limestone gorge, made an irresistible combination. A steep learning curve was had to try to fit all your camping kit in a kayak. Nearby, the Moracca proved more tricky but fun.

On the long drive back north, up the coast, we stopped off for a few days break. On some random day, early evening, I was looking out over the Adriatic with my binoculars. In the far distance, a long way offshore, I could just make out a windsurfer, ever so small. I followed him for a few seconds. A short while later, I spotted him again. But then he was hardly visible. Maybe I was imagining it. Perhaps he just fell off or was having a rest. But I sensed something was wrong. Out came the kayak and tow line. I set off to where I thought I had seen him. Haha, no landmarks just open sea. I reckoned to paddle about 4 km per hour and estimated he was 2 km offshore. Consequently, I resolved to paddle for about 30 minutes.

Thirty-five minutes later, I spotted this guy sitting on his windsurfer, dressed in just his swimming trunks. We were unable to communicate effectively since I was unable to even decipher which language he spoke. All he could say was 'from my friend.' Ah, I spotted a broken mast foot. I showed him how to stow the sail on the board. Clipping the front loop of his board to my towline, we headed ashore, him paddling with hands. The shore looked quite far, but so level was the backdrop of the land, it was tricky to even spot where I had set off from. Hoping there was no current or shore drift, roughly an hour later we landed. The guy was so grateful, he ran up the beach and disappeared with barely a thank you!

My First Expedition

Coruh, Turkey (July 1988)

Sten Sture, Angela Sture, Pip Line,
Chris Walker, Dave Benn, Gareth Walker

Stories in canoeing magazines inspired me. Adventures to unknown foreign climes fired up my imagination.

I had thought of going to Turkey the year before but could not get the necessary team and paperwork sorted out; there was no email in those days, but permits were needed to visit Turkey. Over a few beers at Christmas, I asked Chris and Gareth Walker if they would like to join us on the trip. Chris replied, 'If there is anything I can help with.' He might have regretted his offer as he sorted out the minibus, roof rack and insurance. Slime (Pete Knowles) kindly supplied me with a map, since he had run the river a few years previously. I then invited a few more friends and found a non-paddling driver – Dick Chalmers – who would prove invaluable when we came to moving down the river gorge. We spent almost a week driving to N.E. Turkey.

Friday, 8th

Armed with our Turkish permits, we set off from Cumbria to meet the rest of the team and minibus in Bristol.

Saturday, 9th

From Dover – arrived somewhere in the Black Forest at 3:00 a.m. And slept in a house on a building site. Woken by an earthquake, no it was Dick's snoring.

Sunday, 10th

We drove on to the artificial slalom site at Augsburg, where not having paddled for a few months, we all had fun, even seeing an inflatable palm tree try its luck. We slept in the field on a mountain somewhere in East Austria where the local brown cows moved one of Gareth's flip-flops! Although he thought it more likely it was one of us.

Monday, 11th

Moved south to River Isel where, on a riverside sign, we read the 'inspiring' tale of the death of a British paddler. We floated 21 km from Kalserbach to Lienz. Big and bouncy class 3. This proved to be a good trial for what was to come. We drove on to Yugoslavia where a horse kindly agreed that we could share his field for the night.

Tuesday, 12th

Dave was woken in the night by a hedgehog and blamed it for moving Gareth's flip-flop. Onto the 'death road' and Belgrade, where so many slow, big lorries, two lanes, one horn and no-overtaking rules! go for it. Onward to Greece and a field of straw for the night engulfed by dreams of becoming incorporated in a bale or was it a huge wave?

Wednesday, 13th

Greek farmers woke us with a wave at 6:00 a.m. to swelling on faces and feet – killer ants had attacked. Soon we passed Thessaloniki with its road signs in Greek and we were completely lost. Having guessed our location, we decided to follow a white road on our map of Europe. Soon we were admiring the rough dirt tracks of an unnamed range of hills instead of zooming along the main highway to Turkey. Soon the dirt track became a forest road and after several junctions, we were lost with no map and even worse, no clue. 'We might as well go home then' summed up my frustration. Having retreated, we almost ran out of petrol as the Greeks seemed unaware of Eurocheques. Ten Deutsche Marks left from the Black Forest bought us 10 litres of fuel, enough to get to the Turkish border, where customs officials counted the kayaks and gave us paperwork to be handed in on our return. As we drove on past Istanbul into the night, the police stopped us, and just asked if we were OK. I think we were being tracked.

Thursday, 14th

Breakfast of fresh fruit at 4:00 a.m. then Ankara, the mad roundabout of 6 lanes and 12 sets of traffic lights, then, on and on and on… Stopped by the police again who checked our permit and that we were OK. We rescued a German tourist, by selling him our spare fan belt. The tarmac ran out and the traffic almost disappeared, on and on and on to kebabs and a bivvy out by the Firat Nechi river.

Friday, 15th

We inspected the Firat. It is only class 3 it was tempting, but the lure of the Coruh was strong. Over two more mountain ranges, we arrived at Bayburt with a flat tyre. In this remote village, hiding behind rotten wooden doors that called itself a garage, a smart space-age workshop. The happy mechanic added an inner tube to our flat as we bought food to last us several days.

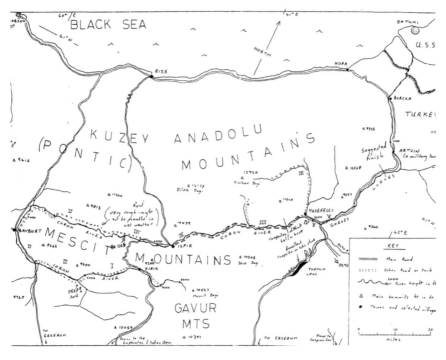

Slime's river map

After seven days of travelling, we finally saw the river Coruh – flat, warm, shallow, foul smelling, low flow and surely infested with disease. What had we come to?

The locals spoke English like the roads had tarmac! The food store offered us tea on the house. Our two ladies, Pip and Angela, thought better of exposing their thighs in public after being trailed by the local youths who mimicked bees to a hive. At 3:00 p.m., a short paddle to stretch the muscles – Dick drove off in the minibus hoping to meet us at the first road bridge; if only he had a map. Animal entrails and rotting fruit floated alongside, down easy water to two weirs where the locals helped and then almost molested the girls back into their boats. At 6:00 p.m., I managed to overbalance my boat while getting in after a portage around the second weir, thus claiming 'River Rat' for the day. We pulled out at the first road bridge at Capci, Coruh. No, Dick! It was only 9 km. Where was he?

A local guy watched us shiver in the cool breeze for 10 minutes before asking 'chi'? Five minutes later, the local lads guarded our boats, as we were led to a small house nearby for 'chi'. Were we about to be kidnapped? The girls were taken away to another room, slightly disconcerting given what they had experienced so far. We learnt, using poor French or maybe just poor understanding, that the Muslim obligation was to help travellers. We were soon warm and a loaf of huge pitta bread and chai were presented to us. Soon the room was full of children, grandparents, relatives and it seemed anyone else who was passing by. Lots of bees in this small village!

Bayburt at start of Courh trip

We chatted away, not understanding very much. The girls were wrapped in blankets and some of our wet clothes were dried by the open fire. More pitta bread and rancid cheese seemed to loosen everyone's bowels, but we never asked for the loo, fearing it to be impolite and dreading the sanitation.

Dick saved the day by turning up 2 hours later. After being confused by the children guarding our boats, we made our thanks and excuses and left. After more food, we played football and frisbee with the locals until one big throw put it in the river. Sten chased the frisbee in his kayak, whilst Chris ran down the bank. The frisbee's attempt at escape was foiled. But this became the source of harmonious laughter between two very different worlds, which turned into an unexpectedly fine welcome to Turkey.

Saturday, 16th

After some discussion with Dick about how he had gotten lost and might need some help finding the next bridge, we were reassured that he was confident in his role.

The river flows through increasingly remote terrain, enhancing the feeling of isolation

We pushed off at 10:00 a.m. for what proved to be a long day. The Coruh, soon swelled by tributaries and small streams, became wider and cleaner. Flowing but only class 1 or 2.

The river flowed across a broad plain in glorious sunshine. Slowly, the mountains became closer. Birdlife flapped in confusion as we passed and local

31

villagers rushed to wave us by, as the sun took its toll on our faces. Games of pooh sticks (no paddling allowed) saw the kilometres drift past.

Gareth chilling out across the plains

Gradually, the river became clearer and small cliffs lined the river bank. Even with only Slime's map, we had no idea where we were, or how far we had to go. Hours more pass when we spot the bridge, a false alarm, just an old ruin.

Into the hills

As dusk approached, we had eaten nothing since lunch at 1:00 p.m. and had run out of potable water. We faced the real prospect of a night out with only the wet clothes we were wearing.

On we went, around the next corner and the next... Seventy kilometres in all. Finally, at 8:00 p.m., a waving Dick sat on a concrete bridge, a goat herder alongside. He looked just like the same guy that we had seen some hours before. Dick recounted tales of his day on the mountain roads, with no signs, with only Slime's map, a few scant villages and no common language, He seriously doubted that he would ever get back to the river. Even then, he was convinced he was at the wrong bridge. The locals mobbed him for hours and even showed him a snake that lived under the bridge.

One local spoke good English but when Dave complimented him 'you speak very good English' he replied 'please, I don't understand' Soon after the locals disappeared, only to return with two loaves of fresh bread and a bag of spring onions.

Sunday, 17th

We estimated our position to be 30 km from Ispir where we expected the 'proper' white water would begin. We were cheered off by the locals who turned out in numbers to see us depart. A few of the more adventurous children hitched a ride on our kayaks, for a few seconds.

Soon after we left, a group of horsemen approached us through the shallow river. They did not look as friendly as all the people we had met so far.

Water taxi!

Giving us mad eyes, they galloped through the shallows towards us. Fortunately, a short sprint and deeper water proved enough to deter their pursuit. The rapids grew in size and some of our team rolled to practice, building their confidence for later. We made Ispir by 1:00 p.m. with Dick waving us to the shore. Around the corner was the first class 4 water.

Slime's map was correct. A quick inspection and we were bobbing down the long rapid with quick turns to avoid nasty rocks and frothing holes.

Chris playing on a wave in the Coruh Gorge

Unfortunately, one of the holes got the better of Gareth and he failed to roll. A short swim later, he zoomed out of the river after seeing a snake swimming near him.

Beautiful and ever-changing scenery all the way

Chris and I followed Gareth's kayak down three more big, bouncy rapids until we secured his Dancer on the right bank – but no sign of his paddles. With only dampened pride Gareth was soon reunited with his kayak but using a spare set of split paddles. We now paddled in pairs, each pair leading in rotation, then waiting as safety cover for the others. The wave trains got longer and bigger and the holes larger. Sten and Dave showed us new tricks.

Dave catches an ender

From Ispir, the road follows the river, so Dick was able to follow us down and indulge in his hobby, photographing our efforts. This meant we could stop whenever we wanted and so an early finish was made.

Driving downstream to inspect the next section, we came across an icy cold mountain stream where we enjoyed a naked wash to rid our bodies of 10 days of grime.

That evening we found Ispir to be a series of dirt streets with open sewers. A Turk, who lived in Belgium, showed us to a restaurant where we indulged in a fine meal with beer. A great end to a great day, or so we thought. As we ate our main course two smartly dressed guys came down the stairs and sat at the table opposite. They waited while we ate, watching us. Fifteen minutes after completing our meal, we were sat on a veranda of the area administrator sipping chai, guarded by armed soldiers. Soon after, we were joined by the chief of police, the director of the town bank, the mayor and an assortment of shopkeepers. It was hard to work out why we were there. It seems we were the guests of honour for the local dignitaries or were we there to pay respect to them? Communication improved somewhat when an English-speaking police sergeant arrived to interpret. We learned about the region and they asked about England. They were most apologetic about their town being so tatty. They were keen to become western and had plans to build seven dams on the river so they could become self-sufficient in electricity.

Back at our tents, a vodka and melon party saw us to sleep.

Monday, 18th

Some went food shopping, the rest sat around in the sun waiting when a shout broke the peaceful sunbathing. There was Gareth's paddle. Running down the steep bank, Chris waded in to retrieve the paddle. Its bent-up metal edge had just caught on a small crystal of rock on a boulder 5 m from the bank.

How amazing! Surely a minor miracle, it had done 4 km and stayed overnight and become stuck just where we camped.

Soon after setting off, the road passed through a tunnel and entered a gorge by the river. The river, sunken in the gorge, varied from class 3 to the odd class 5. The water now more constricted became more turbulent and surging. Some rapids had tight lines through big waves and holes. With only six of the team paddling the others spotted the harder sections from the road. The spotters missed one hard section, so it was paddled on sight, scary! We were lucky to get through without issue. The difficulties eased after a few miles and the girls joined us again for an afternoon of continuous big bouncy class 3 rapids. Our back loop expert Sten showed his skills again. . A superb day's paddle.

Tuesday, 19th

Today the river was bigger with more bouncy wave trains, interspersed with calmer but flowing sections and the odd class 4 line if anyone fancied it.

Sten finding a way through a wave train

Setting up camp and leaving the kayaks by the river, we drove on a mud road to Yusefelli for dinner, which was accompanied by the exceptionally heavy and persistent rain. On the return journey, the road became slippery and then impassable due to mudslides. So an impromptu night in a local hotel provided shelter. An otherwise interesting but undesirable experience caused us to agree that camping to be preferable.

On a swinging footbridge that evening, Sten was enjoying a chill moment with his wife Angela. He was approached by an unkempt local guy, and unexpectedly was challenged to a fight, apparently the prize being Angela.

Wednesday, 20th

We were awoken at some early hour by prayers to Allah being blasted from the mosque just across the street from our hotel. The little mountain stream that wandered gently through the village the night before had turned into a raging brown torrent. As if by magic, from somewhere, two JCB earth movers trundled out of the village to clear the road. It was 3:00 p.m. before we reached our kayaks and our camp. A local offered us apricots and another, sun-dried duts (mulberry I think). We paddled a short while before force six winds blowing upstream combined with brown water brought the day to a halt.

Thursday, 21st

We inspected the main rapids from the road so we could run them without stopping. But remembering all the lines proved difficult as there were eight larger, harder sections. We retreated back upstream to the previous day's end and began on the brown swollen water.

Into the first big rapid, it was too late. We soon realised that the main problem was not being able to see the breaking water which normally would be white, but with so much sediment in the river, the holes and breaking waves became brown, indistinguishable from the flatter water - like a chocolate brown out.

Paddling on instinct became the name of the game.

The last section of Hades

Dave practising his chocolate roll

Chris describes an MOT, his experience on the third rapid of the day, which shows the importance of confidence. *"A small tongue offered the least horrific option between two enormous stoppers and exploding waves. On the water, I found I could not see the tongue. As I craned my neck I found myself too far right and realised with horror that I was dropping straight into a big hole that I had intended to miss at all costs. I dug hard with my paddle and powered into the wave nervous energy helping. The lights went out as I was submerged in the brown wave, then came back on again. I was on the top of the recirculating wave and managed to briskly paddle off to find myself straight into the next hole. I used a big support stroke on the brown froth saw me through. Then a fantastic bit of steering to miss the next one and I was in control again. I was through, despite my mistakes. Slowly I relaxed as the fear ebbed from my hands to be replaced by enjoyment on my face. If I could make that sort of mistake and still come through, the rest must be easy."*

And so it was, the next rapids came and went in a similar vein. Until we reached the confluence with the Oltu. The Coruh was brown but when mixed with the sediment-saturated Oltu river, only flowing chocolate can be an accurate description. The gorge air filled with the scent of fresh soil.

Thick brown water washed over our kayaks, depositing small piles of mud. Clay clung to the paddles, making them slippery to hold. Fortunately, the section was easier but you could never feel completely at ease.

Hades, one of the eight big rapids after Yusefelli

The minibus had stopped at what we called Hades. Many lines were discussed but even the easiest involved bursting through huge angled stoppers. It seemed to require more bottle than we were prepared to give. Combined with the problems of reading the chocolate-coloured water we decided this was a fitting point to end the paddle. Humility had defeated our aim of paddling to the coast without a portage.

With some sadness, we loaded the boats on the minibus and headed for the Black Sea coast just 12 miles from Russia.

We found a little restaurant and ordered fresh fish, out of a tank, fish along with lots of beer to celebrate. The owner joined us for more beer but became bemused when Gareth put a waterproof match in his beer, and then lit it. Gareth then gave him an ordinary match which, of course, would not light. Free raki all round, but a big one for Gareth. He refused to drink it until the owner had balanced three beer glasses on each other. Shared laughter accompanied the cracking of glasses. Gareth drank the raki. We slept on the beach by the restaurant.

The next five days saw us drive along the black sea coast, having a surf competition, rescuing a tortoise, throwing rocks at dogs in the middle of the night to frighten them off and buying 5 kg of cheese. Gareth complained as he did not like cheese. Subsequently, the cheese turned out to be marzipan – lovely with Branston pickle! Gareth kept laughing, constantly winding us up; until we dampened his mirth by taking a break and introducing him to a small river. He also complained and became frustrated as our insurance had declared that he was too young to drive the minibus. This was a fair point since he was the only one whose job involved driving them.

Somewhere in Yugoslavia, we bought him a carton of Gris, dried baby food, as compensation.

Wednesday, 27th

We arrived late at the river Una in Bosnia and Herzegovina where we had decided to break the journey. We tried asking the locals about Strabacki Buk a waterfall on the Una that we had read about in our German DKV guidebook. They pointed over the hills so we guessed there was no road to the falls.

Our plan to buy food in the local village fell flat so dinner became all the leftovers.

Thursday, 28th

A tin of mandarins, mixed with Gareth's packet of Gris did not go far between eight for breakfast. The Una proved to be a long paddle. The water was flat and then flat and pancake, hardly flowing. The guidebook mentioned 30m falls. Three hours later, just around the next corner, the current gained pace as a faint roar could be heard. There they were, the crystal clear falls of Strabacki Buk in all their glory.

Sten above and the author below on Strabacki Buk, River Una

We portaged the main 10 m drop (it is paddled these days) which leads to further a 4 m drop, which we ran a few times. Then it continued into a small 2 km long limestone gorge with more small falls and narrow slides and class 3 rapids eventually widening into a wide flat section.

A typical ledge on the Una

Class 3 ledges entertained us between long flat sections where terrapins sunbathed. We finally reached Dick and the minibus at 3:00 p.m. having not eaten food nor water since 8:00 a.m.

The whole of this trip to Turkey cost us only £200, including the minibus hire fuel and food. We had been self-sufficient on the river and gained a real sense of adventure and exploration. The journey down the river had been helped by having Dick drive the minibus. The element of the journey was an intrinsic part of the trip. The river scenery was stunning and the paddling had a good variety, yet challenging enough to make the adrenaline run. At times the difficulties proved very pushy, yet even the odd portage added a feeling of humility, that seemed to complement the success of the trip. Finding a way through a country that we knew little about had proved an enjoyable and rewarding challenge. The Turkish people were very friendly, giving us gifts and smiling all the time.

Back at home, it was with some comfort and pride that you could look at an atlas and draw a long line along the route we had followed.

Such a fun exploration. With the concept planned and then brought to a successful and rewarding conclusion. So satisfying.

I had to have more.

Bigger Still

Colorado, Grand Canyon (August 1987)

Robin Everingham, Andy Hall

What a summer! Two weeks after arriving home from paddling on the Coruh in Turkey, I was getting off a plane at Flagstaff, Arizona, intending to descend the Grand Canyon of the Colorado River. The previous year, I had been speaking to Robin Everingham about paddling trips when the Grand Canyon came up in conversation. Were we good enough we wondered? Only one way to find out! We were going to put our name on the list for getting a permit for running the river. Having discovered that it was so popular, to avoid a wait time of 15 years, we booked on to a commercial trip with Dick McCallum's company Expeditions Inc. Because of my trip to Turkey and Robin's other plans, our time frame did not coincide with the start of a full trip in one go, so we arranged to meet the rafts halfway down the river.

Huge walls of sedimentary layers

We aimed to walk down the Bright Angel trail into the canyon, then paddle from river mile 88 to the end, a few days rest, then paddle the upper 0-88 mile, and then walk back out.

An iconic river, the Colorado has its own rapid grading system from 1 to 10 and most rapids are named. Technical paddling skills of grade 10 being equivalent to 4 on the normal scale.

Having met the raft team after a 4 hour hike down the Bright Angel trail we started with a bang. A few bends brought us to Pipe Springs (4) and then to our baptism in Horn Creek (8).

Horn Creek – we thought this was big. But!

Some might say an interesting baptism. What the grades do not tell is the size of the waves – exploding waves. Horn Creek leads straight into Granite (10).

I had thought the Coruh had big water, but at 20000 cfs this was something else.

Robin in Granite

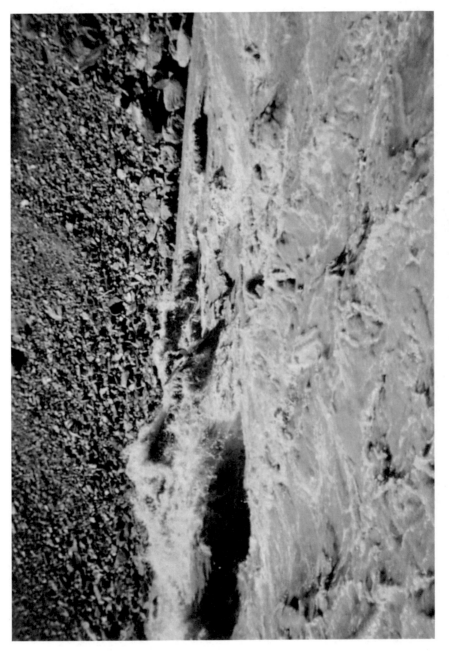

The waves in Hermit – how big! with unpredictable explosions

47

Robin in Crystal

The main problem with our plan is that two of the biggest four rapids in the canyon, Crystal and Granite were just after our put-in. In the first seven miles, we would have three of the four grade 8-10 rapids. The river was brown - memories of the Coruh returned but gave me confidence rather than concern.

The water that flows down the Grand Canyon from the bottom of Glen Canyon dam. 15 miles upstream the water is clear, and almost icy cold, in great contrast to the 40°C+ heat in the air. The flow volume changes according to Hydroelectric power demand. So pulses of higher 20000 cfs and lower water 8000 cfs run along the canyon. You go to sleep at lower water, in the morning it can be two feet higher, or vice versa, depending on how far downstream you are from the dam.

Soon, the first biggie, Granite (10), my run went well until a wave exploded, consuming me, MOT, it went ever so dark! *brace! Lean on the breaking wave, I told myself, and keep the pressure on my paddle.* I rotated 360^0 back to upright, having done a roll without trying. What a buzz!

As if that wasn't a good enough introduction, next we found Hermit (9) on full flow, which had the plus there was a good eddy, a big eddy, so you could float back upstream and do it again and again and again…We found such a big standing wave, 3 kayaks long, always changing, sometimes smooth. Occasionally the front exploded, intimidating, but surfing it was so rewarding, tantalising enough to want the perfect surf, we couldn't resist repeating the buzz gained by surfing the face of this monster.

Three more miles to absorb the river, the canyon walls and adrenaline brought us to Crystal (10). Lines of huge stoppers, either side of a nightmare huge hole of FWD. Paddle with momentum, brace lots, then some more bracing and hope for the best, proved a successful tactic.

After the high of making it past the stoppers, I was soon brought back down by the eddy line below, on most rivers a calm place to rest. Not here, my eddy boiled up and down by two feet and was no place to wait; the river had other ideas about allowing escape. The boils extracted two rolls, from me before I made the 'calmer' water in the real eddy just downstream.

Having made it through Granite and Crystal, we were now in tune with the river and the rest, as they say, was a blast. Only about 10% of the 200-mile run is white water. Between are mellow, but still fast-flowing stretches. Imagining a way up the cliffs, gazing at the bedding planes in the rock strata intermixed with many riffles, each of which allowed endless surfing and picking routes through enormous water, became the routine. Many riffles allowed endless surfing.

Since we had raft support for our trip, the food was fantastic: eggs any way you like to start the day, a wild assortment of cheeses, salami and salads for lunch, with steak and halibut done on a charcoal grill for dinner. Time seems to standstill. The only measure of progress is miles covered, which slowly decreases to the end. The canyon slowly grabs you so you feel part of it. The world could be at war – you would have no idea. The canyon and the river become more than a holiday or just another river trip. It becomes a way of life.

The 40°C air temperature contrasts with the 4°C of the water. The still arid desert-like shore conflicts with the brown turbulence rushing past. The 12 days of our seemingly big adventure is dwarfed by millions-of-year-old geomorphology. A place to wander and lose yourself in. The river and the canyon, it is all-absorbing.

We stop every so often to break the paddling and hike for an hour or two up a side canyon marvelling at the natural water sculpture of tight gorge walls. Sandstone in bands of orange, brown or ochre, or Travertine limestone.

The odd scorpion keeps you wary when ashore whilst antlions wait in their shallow inverted conical pits. Our trip allows time to relax, forget and float in a bubble, knowing that no one can help - you simply rely on your own skills and resources.

Days later, it's Lava (10) the big daddy rapid. Another nightmare hole with FWD in the middle. Left a series of unpredictably variable stoppers, right vague tongue between huge boils leads into 3 sides of huge collapsing walls, a proverbial dead end.

Author in Lava

Wow, what a choice. Best try to go right, to the dead end, underneath the final wave. Will it go? YESSSS. *Focus on what is just in front, and try and recognise those breaking waves as markers. Stay calm, adrenaline winning, heart rushing, move left then right, until just upstream of the ever-changing tongue. It sucks you forward, into the corridor where the walls fall in breaking confusion. The end is big, much bigger than it looked from scouting on the bank high above, ever so big. I have no idea which way to brace, big folding waves fall into the corridor from both sides, the end a wall of FWD, paddle faster to gain speed, lean forward and hope not to be back looped. What happened next is all rather random and incomprehensible, but then I am through, burst the back wall and shriek with relief, can smiles get bigger?* YESSSSS

We walked back up and run the left side too.

Occasionally, we meet on other raft trips, but not so many. Some ride super rafts–35' monsters with huge engines. At the first encounter, you just feel it is strange, just invaders who pollute the canyon with their noise and diesel fumes. Running the whole canyon in 3 days, which surely misses the whole essence of the journey. To be honest, it detracts from the serenity and wildness that is the canyon. But fortunately not for long. For them, it is just a matter of a tick 'I've done the canyon' slotted into a long weekend in a hectic life.

Robin and I return to civilisation for just one day before we returned to start the second part of our trip. It was a welcome rest, but, to be honest, rather spoiled the continuity of the absorbing journey, the ethos of the canyon was interrupted.

The following evening we were glad to be looking out at the start of the canyon at Lees Ferry for the first 88 miles of the Canyon. The river had captured our minds. The following morning in a haze of sleep and sunrise Robin spots a floater, 'badger' he shouts. Of course, he meant beaver! We laughed as a log floated by. A few more badgers accompanied our giggling through the following days. Andy Hall had joined and almost left us as he insisted on walking the parapet of the bridge, hundreds of metres above the canyon, just downstream.

The first half of the gorge, our second half, was easier to enjoy. I knew the hardest rapids were behind us, downstream! Buoyed by the confidence that we had coped well. The water was clear; our fitness good and we had learnt new skills for dealing with huge waves. Andy Hall joined the trip. Generally, it was playtime. About day 3, at mile 61.5, we reached the Little Colorado river junction. A tributary, heavily laden with silt and sand, it flowed at a low volume but was tainted with a deep brown colour. At first, the clear green-blue of the main river pushed the brown invader to the left bank. However, with a high sediment burden, the intruder gradually mixed, until a few miles later the whole river became tainted. It stayed that way for the rest of the 180 miles. This was desert country, so despite the hot days, the nights were chilly, with no clouds to retain the day's heat. The roller coaster chill of the river is never far away. We often bivvied out on a sandy beach.

This worked well until one night it was warmer, and clouds filled the evening sky. We awoke to drizzle. Breakfast was taken in chilly thick fog. Setting off on the river, unable to see more than 20 m ahead was rather worrying. The raft guides suggested that there were no big rapids to worry us. With cold hands today, as I floated off, I discovered that the best way to warm my hands was to outstretch my arms, hold the paddle, horizontally above my head, where it protruded from the fog into the warm sun, cold face, warm hands; weird. The guides were correct: the river was an easy float. An hour or so later, the hot rising sun evaporated the fog. Enthralled by the rapids, literally captivated by the walls - floating the river becomes your life, a totally absorbing experience.

Robin pulling an ender

The PRAT Scale

The Personal Rapid Assessment Test

The PRAT scale is a mechanism for estimating if you should attempt to paddle a rapid or fall. The most important aspect of deciding to run a fall or rapid is that it is your own decision. As long as you paddle to the level of your competence and not past it, into misadventure, you will challenge and enjoy yourself. With more experience, your estimate of your ability will be close to your current level of competence. With less experience, you will have difficulty assessing the objective dangers and possible consequences. If your assessment of your ability and the intricacies of rapid or fall is inaccurate, you may well pass the threshold of adventure, thus entering the realms of misadventure unless luck intervenes. Misadventure can have serious consequences, even death. The closer you get to the line of misadventure the more heightened the buzz will be. As your skills improve you will likely need more challenge, to get the same buzz. This, of course, means that the objective dangers are more serious.

More horizontal rapids are generally easier to judge than vertical falls. But a whole river is rarely the same grade all the way. The present grading system relies on describing the water features. Perhaps this is the wrong way of looking at it, as this only gives an indication of the water features, not the skills required to paddle. Of course, this relies on the paddler knowing what the grades mean or being guided by a more experienced friend. An alternative system could reflect the skills needed in paddling each grade. This sort of description would tell the inexperienced grade 3 paddler that grade 4 probably isn't for them as they don't have precise and accurate control of the boat at all times. When I wrote my paddling guidebook 'The Rivers of Cumbria' I tried to rationalise to myself the reasons why you might grade a river a particular grade. I added F for larger falls and W for weirs, offering no grade, thus expecting each paddler to self-assess the situation at the time of paddling. Which of course you should be doing all the time anyway.

Grade	Paddling skills needed
1	No real skill is needed. You can simply float down.
2	Directional control needed to follow easy routes
3	Some precise manoeuvring is required, use of support strokes can be expected.
4	Precise and accurate control of the boat is needed at all times. The ability to use the water to help navigation is needed. The ability to roll to avoid a swim is desirable.
5	Some submerging of either end or the whole kayak can lead to the need to constantly correct the course of the boat. The ability to 'see' the route even when submerged or capsized. The ability to support in unexpected waves and roll the first time is essential.
6	Ability to react with speed and instinct to ever rapidly changing situations. You can expect to have to hang on in there even on a good run. If you cannot follow the desired route death may occur.

The PRAT scale includes the factors that might influence your decision when deciding to run a rapid or fall. Use the PRAT scale to assess whether or not you should run a particular fall or rapid by simply combining your + and – scores as outlined in this table. The less experienced will get lower (more negative scores) than the more experienced.

At home, try it out for the last rapid or fall you had a problem with or that you portaged. Total your score for yourself, for that rapid on that day, in the same conditions that existed. You won't recall all this on the river but it is good to ask yourself these questions, it might just tweak your thinking.

Factor to consider	Score	
A. Yourself		
1. What grade of water do you normally paddle successfully?	Grade 3	0
	Grade 4	1
	Grade 4/5	2
	Grade 5+	3
	Grade 6	6
2. How many years have you been Paddling?	More than 6	2
	More than 3	1
	Less than 3	−1
	Less than 1	−3
3. Have you recently paddled	A lot	2
	A bit	1
	Rusty	0
	Not a lot	−1
B. Environment		
4. Estimated grade of rapid (1–6)	Up to 6	−1 for each grade
5. Is river in spate?	No	0
	Yes	−1
6. Does the rapid contain potholes, undercuts, sumps, overhanging trees or branches, small fall with shallow rocks, high falls or very large volume?	For each of these Present	−1
7. Is the rapid in an inescapable gorge?	Yes	−1
	No	0
8. Is the air (water) temperature?	More than 20°C	1
	Less than 5°C	−1

Factor to consider	Score	
9. Can you be easily rescued if the need arises?	Yes	1
	No	−1
10. Length of trip so far?	Less than 2 hours	1
	More than 3 hours	−1
C. Experience		
11. Do you think you have successfully paddled a rapid as hard as this one?	Yes	0
	No	−2
12. Have you paddled this rapid before at this water level?	Yes	2
	No	−1
13. Did you inspect the rapid and could clearly see it?	Yes	1
	No	−1
D. The group		
14. Has anyone ever successfully paddled this rapid before?	Yes	1
	No	−1
15. Has anyone in your group done the rapid on the day?	No	−1
	Yes, they were successful score 1 per person up to a maximum of 5	1-5
16. Did the probe make the rapid look easy?	Yes	1
	No	−1
17. What is your feel-good factor?	Looks good	2
	Probably OK	1
	Not sure	−1
	Looking dubious	−2

The more positive your score the more likely you will run the rapid successfully. A negative score indicates that a portage might be advisable. The more negative your score the riskier an attempt would be (the more likely you are to be a prat). I have tried it out and it seems to work for me.

Anyone for Tees

Low Force Right side

On were on the way to play a kayak polo match for Lakeland Canoe Club, in Darlington. We decided to visit the Upper Tees. It was February. The water level was low but paddleable. Hard frozen snow lay about. The river was mostly frozen too, but enough clear water flowed between the frozen, icy shelves to allow us to make progress. The section to Low Force is a few hundred metres of class 4 that leads to the drop of Low Force.

Right, a vertical 3 m drop; left, a steep slide into a boil, formed as the water rebounds off the rocky cliff jutting out onto the flow. The base was mostly frozen except for a narrow 2-boat-width wide channel.

Just 50 m below Low Force another rapid into a narrower gorge, where the ice sat solid, wall to wall. No way through.

Better not swim down there.

Low Force left side – Chilly

In some strange way, the exhilaration of the fall was enhanced by the chill of the water. Exciting and refreshing!

Extending the Challenge

The Tarn Gorges, Central Massif France
(April 1988)
Gareth Walker, Ken Gowler,
Andy Westlake, Pip Line

It was almost by accident that we found ourselves in Florac. We had been to the Ardeche and spent a long day paddling down the stunning but mostly grade 1 gorge. We had found more excitement on the upper Ardeche, but the flows in the main tributaries were too low, so we decided to head west to the Tarn to find more rivers to paddle, with no particular aims in mind. What a fortuitous decision it turned out to be. The campsite in Florac was frequented by many German paddlers. With their RV's decked out to carry 4 kayaks and a family. This was clearly the place to be. After some difficulties with translating strange conversations, we soon had a list of rivers to attempt.

Nearby, the lower Tarn gorge to Florac entertained us with bedrock granite and boulder-choked rapids. At 8 km, class 3 and one class 4, it seemed to fit the bill. The section also benefited from ending at our campsite. The following morning saw us descend this fantastic section from La Vernede with blue skies and lots of wow moments. The granite slabs, play waves and crystal-clear water gave us such a buzz, and so raised our confidence – this is what we had been looking for. The gauge when we finally found it halfway down the section read 228 or maybe 128. A good level.

Consulting our German DKV guidebook, the upper Tarn Gorge from Pont de Montvert seemed to offer more of the same. 'When the going gets tough, the tough get going.'

Tarn gorge, Pont de Montvert at the top
Attributed Google Earth

The upper Tarn is 8 km, graded 4–5 if you miss out on the first 2 km graded 5-6. But starting from road marker 43.2 meant carrying the kayaks down the side of the gorge for 120 m. Well, it was that, or do 2 km of 5-6. After much discussion between valour and discretion, the latter won through. The adventure began. Out with the tow lines and rescue ropes; we lowered our kayaks down the steep wooded gorge side; bit by bit. During the descent, Andy slid over a rocky outcrop when his boat hit him from behind and then bashed him into a tree. Fortunately, his only injury was a cut under his left eye. As we descended adrenaline levels rose. What were we doing? PFE to be sure.

Looking down the Tarn gorge. The first rapid you see is the 'Trumpet'

We had arrived at the river just below the 'trumpet'. A good thing too, we agreed; it is a long slide in a narrow slot into a deep hole. Chris described it as *"Deathville warmed up"* Thoughts of that *"Looks interesting"* would have to wait for future visits or as Chris put it *"As interesting as Custer's last stand"*. We made it all the way to the second rapid, about 150 m before Ken had to roll. The river was pool drop, literally drop, pool, then another drop. (Those of you that are familiar with the river Etive in Scotland will know the type. Only this is 6 km!).

Sometimes more pool and other times more drop. I was buzzing, this would be a fun challenge.

The second 1.8 m fall below the trumpet

Soon after, a tight 1.8 m drop, with a right angle turn into a high bubbleosity pool, heralded the start of what we called the 'cornet'.

A 3 m wide rift 300 m long, with 5 small drops and a big slide at the end. This was the first of the harder sections, which we ran one at a time. Unfortunately, for Andy, it became what he claimed to be 'his best attempt at drowning'. On the second drop, he didn't have enough speed. Consequently, he was sucked back into the stopper, followed by an impressive back loop. This is totally disorientating, so Andy decided a dose of ITS was his best chance. We had positioned rescuers with throw lines along the rift, but at every drop, Andy disappeared from sight under the stoppers. His impression of a rag doll on the final slide was quite like squeezing ice cream out of the bottom of a cone.

The final pool was so shallow and he was able to sit there, regain his breath and eventually, his sense of humour as we reunited him with his paddle and boat, which had decided to play in one of the stoppers on its own.

Typical Tarn, Gareth slides a tight drop.

Our team of 4 were all tested to the limits. Many difficult and complicated drops and slides followed. Most were fun, but some were very serious.

Frequently, an inspection was needed to find a paddleable line, to see the hazards, and then portage around or paddle it. This is where your skills improve, they have to. Four hours later we had only covered 4 km. There were simple falls into flat pools, and slides that ran into more slides. At one point a boulder split the river flow, the right side would cause a 'backender' whereas the left was easier. But we never knew what was coming, being probe proved scary but fun. We arrived at the section, which looked just impossible. A cliff jutted out into the river, just where the river flowed over, around and under boulders. If you could find a way on, what was around the corner? Long necks shrank, and long legs pulled the boats up over and around, yet again.

A longer portage around two very narrow rocky drops forced us to take a rest and a bite to eat. Mars bars never tasted so good. It was 3:00 p.m. and we were knackered, but with the only option, to continue. Luck was on our side. The pools started to become more common than the falls, and the drops were technically easier, although still, more than 12 needed inspecting.

An hour or so later after a loop in the river course on an innocuous slab, the front of my dancer kayak came down hard on a slab and split.

What a place for this to happen. One broken boat. In my repair kit, I had a roll of plumbers tape. A few wraps of this solved the problem. The final 4 km took only 2.5 hours.

Individually, we each made between 8, and 14 portages, collected some swims and grazed knuckles. Many times we got stuck on rocks, but in our own way we survived the day, challenged physically and mentally. As a team, we won through, simply brilliant. I decided I like event horizons (you can see the edge but not what is below). But we knew that we could do better.

Wider Horizons

Sun Kosi – Nepal (December 1998)

John Hough, Pip Line, Colin Unwin, Chris Dickinson

A local lad shows us the way

Having tried Europe, it seemed natural to spread the net a bit wider. A chance trip to Nepal, along the Sun Kosi and then 2 days on the Trisuli river seemed to fit the bill. To be honest, it transpired that paddling was not that difficult, but the idea of travelling for a week, a journey, on the same river plus one with a bigger volume, grabbed my imagination. I booked onto a trip, just to cut out all the hassle and admin in Kathmandu. The Sun Kosi was more memorable for the big wave trains, simple enough to float down as long as you are prepared for the unexpected exploding wave, by your side or even from underneath you. Although the river flows through a remote valley, whenever we stopped, local villagers seemed to appear from everywhere. We became the objects of interest in the zoo; with the locals just standing there and watching our every move. After a while, this became disconcerting – but tolerance was the only way to deal with it.

Day 4 of the trip was Christmas eve. It brought us to the first of some bigger rapids.

A mellow section on the Sun KosiChose

At lunchtime, '*What do you fancy for dinner?*' asked the raft guide, '*Chicken would be nice.*' He wandered off to the local village. A big fat chicken joined us. When we all refused to stuff the clucking bird into the back of our kayak, it was tied by its feet to the top of the already overloaded raft.

Each rapid was accompanied by squawking and flapping. It seems the bird was just as anxious as us judging by the piles of guano that became deposited on our dry bags.

The kilometres passed, and we saw no one. Only the evidence of deforestation hints at the presence of humans. The remoteness of the river seemed to be no defence against deforestation by the locals for firewood, with many hillsides being devoid of trees. I wondered what will they use in the future.

We ran most of the rapids on sight. Harkapur is the exception. A longer confused rapid with lots of pour-overs to avoid. Interestingly we all chose very different routes to each other, all finding a way through this long complicated rapid.

Harkapur rapid, Sun Kosi

The following day was Christmas day. That evening, a young goat was brought to visit. Nice! This is dinner, Oh! Hours later it was goat momos, with rice and veg. The meat was so tough. We felt obligated to eat it all though since the beast had been sacrificed just for us. Maybe just rice and veg next time.

The raft guide Putchi told us that many precious stones have been found in the river. So that evening when the moon shone brightly, we saw reflections from the river bed. Not too deep, so we waded in, guided by those still standing on the shore. After 20 minutes of searching, we gave up after finding only a quartz crystal, unsure if the story was genuine or a ruse.

Spider monkeys, baboons, snowy egrets and several species of Kingfisher waved, squawked or howled as we passed by. The following morning Pip feels ill and vomits the previous night's dinner on the sandy beach.

As the sun rose, a few pigs emerged from the houses nearby. Oh no! oh yes! Well, yes! Maybe that's where the phrase as sick as a pig comes from.

Back on the river, there are more big rolling rapids to play in or are they playing with you? We took the opportunity to surf some wave trains.

Misty morning

Exploding waves knock you off course

Deciding that it was a good plan to head back upstream on one such train Colin pulled an ender, with a twist. Or maybe it was the river playing with him.

Nice one Colin

Then all too soon, we reach the confluence of the Tamur. The smell of the Indian terai beyond wafted up the river bound on the southerly breeze. The trip is over. The bus ride was an 18-hour slog back to Kathmandu. Time to reflect and gather thoughts on the various aspects of the journey as well as the challenge and adventure.

A few days later the Trisuli proved to be more of a beast. The water was low since much of the snow that fed it was locked up in the snowpack of the Himalayas. However, there was still enough volume of water to form large class 4 rapids as the water flows over a steeper boulder-strewn river bed.

Close miss of a munchy hole

The Trisuli is renowned for its long trains of large breaking waves. There are so many of these. You just go for it and deal with what comes. From the crest of each wave, you quickly learn to look well ahead. You plan to miss the worst of what you can see, but inevitably you can't avoid it all. Every moment was tense until you are safely in an eddy, at the end of each long section. You then wondered why you fussed! In truth almost all lines were OK.

In one rapid, a huge boulder diverged the flow. As the water converged again downstream, a small whirlpool is formed. In my long kayak, I was able to sit on the rotating water, spin around with the whirlpool, until the energy was dissipated.

We swapped kayaks.

In a shorter kayak like a Rotobat, the experience became all the more wonderful. The sucking downforce of the whirlpool proved stronger than the upward force of buoyancy provided by the kayak, so as I span around you sank. My head was level with the water and then sank more, so you could in effect see the sky through a hole in the water. It was just like being flushed down a plug hole, until the buoyancy won and you accelerated up, exploding like a ballistic missile.

Through the application of previously acquired skills, in this new dynamic, I felt I was both technically and emotionally prepared to deal with the possible consequences of what was to come.

Sunset and Venus

Exploring at Home

Allt Chaorainn, River Etive
Tributary, Scotland (Various Dates)
Dave Hansen, Steve Hansen

The slabs

We chose a fabulous sunny weekend in May. Armed with a video camera, we went to make our first kayaking movie. The water level was low but perfect. We were able to film the main run as we progressed in the morning and the Dalness Falls section in the afternoon. Given the perfect conditions, we decided to take a look at a small tributary, the Allt Chaorainn. A 15-minute carry uphill proved a bit of a challenge, but rewarding us with virgin granite slabs, with just enough water flowing. I had the bug and had a keen group of friends equally excited to find more challenges. I visited mid-Scotland, mid-Wales and the Pennines, mostly running known rivers, but occasionally, we struck lucky and found new sections to explore.

Steeper

Dave – the final chimney drop of Allt Chaorainn

Dillw, Upper Ystwyth

2nd fall Aysgarth, river Ure

Improving the Odds

Tarn Gorges (April 1989 and 1990)

Colin Unwin, Gareth Walker, Ken Gowler,
Andy Westlake, Piers Nesbit, Spike Green,
Steve Lawrence, Nige, Tom, the ambulance man

The lure was simply too great. We had thought we could do better, so we went back the following year. It would also be better to include the first 2 km of the Tarn gorge and decrease the number of portages. I had spent the previous summer exploring new rivers in Yugoslavia, Italy and Austria and I had been to the Sun Kosi and Trisuli rivers in Nepal.

The river level was lower these two years, so the stoppers were less sucky but the falls rockier and the pools shallower. As a paddler, this meant that you could be more relaxed but on occasion, you had to take more angled lines or boof to prevent going so deep at the bottom of a drop, otherwise known as 'pancaking (landing flat) off a FLW'.

Braver now, with more experience and only good memories of the river we headed for Le Pont de Montvert where the upper section (2 km grade 5-6) started. Four hundred metres of boulders brought us to some shallow slabs which led in 200 m to the first event horizon. The way on OTI, trickier to paddle than it looks. Chris hit the cushion fell in and half rolled up, but enough to get him to the bow of Richard's boat, which he was able to use to right himself. Gareth argued with the gorge monsters. They tipped him in, trapped his paddle underwater and saw him swim, whereby he lost his glasses. Round one to the river.

Credit due though, despite not being able to see the river properly he paddled on!

Next came another event horizon. I went right and scraped my knuckles on the rock before disappearing up to the armpit in bubbles before being spat out.

Piers went left, did a back-ender and skyrocketed out of the water. This gave the others a choice, what a choice.

Just around the corner the river the start of the first real DIB! A hard series of cushions and boulders in a narrow channel looked hard. We were tempted to try until closer inspection found a just submerged boulder blocking the way at a 90° bend. Disappointed but also relieved, the decision was made for us.

Seal launch next to the French Horn

Next, a huge cascade. Imagine sliding down the roof of your house, into your garden -then you have it - The 'French Horn'- bigger than the 'Trumpet' that we had seen the previous year. If you didn't fancy the Horn you could seal launch instead. This time we all opted for the seal launch.

It was probably easier paddling the fall, but with my mind made up it is never a good idea to change it. So the boats went up over a small cliff and across some steep slabs before perching on a sloping narrow ledge, whilst you put on your spray deck, holding your paddle just in case!

Trumpet just after the entrance slide – Bobsleigh run

The next significant obstacle was the 'Trumpet, the fall we had started below the previous year. Gareth, by this time, was in no mood to tackle it. The myth of this fall had built from when we had first seen this the previous year. There is only one way to deal with a myth dispel it. *At the entrance, you find your way through a maze of boulders, tricky enough in its own right. Then slide over some small drops, avoid getting pushed off-course by inconsistent boils, followed by a drop into the angry slot. Edge on the cushions as the water slides you inevitably to the bobsleigh run. The decibels increase, and on to the final long chute. As you reach the top. Smile- a big smile - accelerate 10m, hold your breath, just before submarining, completely disappearing under the stopper.*

Open your eyes, and suddenly, everything is blue and silent, seeing bubbles rise, all is calm and silent. Your mind grabs the diverse emotions of the moment. Under the stopper and through into the calm pool below.

What a buzz!

Custer's last stand was claimed, even by Chris.

The author taking the Trumpet

Spike running the Trumpet

Trumpet from downstream

This upper 2 km had taken 2 hours. But now we were on more familiar water, albeit at a slightly lower volume.

Not long after the trumpet, a 2.5 m fall leads to a rocky rapid and a very tight right turn. OTI, from above looked fine! Or miss it and you are in trouble. Gareth missed, then glanced off the rock in the drop, and within seconds was pinned, trapped underwater.

Gareth takes the final drop of a set of three, just before he gets pinned

This pin completed his hat trick of misfortune for the day. Richard was closest and sprang into action, grabbing Gareth's outstretched hand and pulling him free. Retrieving the boat was less easy. It involved Colin diving in, to fix a line to the boat's bow, and then, with five of us pulling, it became free. Gareth was full of praise for his kayak design with its bulkhead footrest and wide keyhole cockpit. Total respect for him, he just slid back into his kayak and was keen to continue.

The rest of the trip was more or less straightforward except that Tom took some unusual lines, in fact, some that I would not attempt if you paid me. That evening back on the campsite, whilst recounting the tales of the day, Tom's version, about his skill level and route choice, changed with each beer consumed. We managed the 8 km in only 4 hours. I had managed to do the complete trip with only 3 portages and was pleased with my efforts.

French horn from the top – Richard slides down the roof

In 1990, yet again, we were lured to the Upper Tarn. This year was memorable for two runs down the gorge on consecutive days. After the dreams and dramas of the previous attempts at the gorge, it was comforting to recall how much detail of so many drops and lines you can remember. Starting at Pont de Montvert again with a similar water level to the previous year. The initial granite boulders bring back good memories for me, the trigger of delight. This time we were not to be defeated. A big MOT on top of the 'French Horn' I sit above a great slab. The pool, I know, is below, but I just can't see it. I hear the roar and I can smell the fine spray rising to the top. This time, the lure is too great to resist. The water is going somewhere indeterminate down the 'roof'. My brain says no, the adventurer in me says go. *I push off, immediately regretting your choice, too late. Edge left, a paddle stroke to gain some speed, then another to boof off the lip; let gravity have its way, only my balance to help. A concatenation of a blurred shower, a big dipper ride feeling and adrenaline. I brace for the impact with the water, but it does not come. Instead, I gently sink into the cushion of bubbles of the frothy surface below, like landing on a cushion. Before I know it, I am looking back up, wanting to do it again.* Our small team saw us crack the French Horn and complete the whole 8 km gorge in only 3.5 hours with two portages.

We had improved! That evening some 6 friends arrived, so the following day we did it all again. I was so pleased not to be one of the lemmings. All credit to them for just following and believing our descriptions and just going for it.

French Horn

On our first trip down the Tarn Gorge 6 km from the Trumpet, it took almost 6 hours, with 8 portages for me. Five runs and three years later, I had improved the odds. Now I 'knew' the river from Pont de Montvert, the 8 km had taken only 4 hours with only 2 portages. We had been bolder, we had improved, and my line of misadventure moved up.

Scrimblies

Like me, you have probably been mystified by some of the things that happen to you when you are out paddling on the river.

Paddling down the lower section of the river Clough in Cumbria, one day in February, I wasn't concentrating and so drifted into a tree. Innocent enough until I felt my head wrenched back by the tree as the end of a broken branch penetrated one of the slits in my Wild Water helmet. As I drifted past, the tree branch developed a bend and so tension in its branch, until, at the crucial point the branch did not break but took revenge on my carelessness and propelled me back upstream.

On another occasion, whilst on the river Ger in the Pyrenees. We had a short but delicate paddle down a narrow tree-strewn gorge with an emphasis on avoiding the boulders liberally strewn on the steep bedrock. Having successfully negotiated many such rapids for a kilometre or so, we came to a pool under a road bridge. It was flat and still, with no evidence of obstruction. Four others passed across the pool without incident. But as I drifted across, I stopped on a spike of rock, hidden just under the surface, which seemed to appear from nowhere. A 7 cm slice cut through the plastic of my Corsica kayak, underneath the seat. I slowly began to sink. I sometimes paddle with a dog's tail on the rear end of my boat to help me should I get pinned on rocks. On one occasion, my dog's tail managed to tie itself around a piece of wood caught in the river bed. This left me stationary in the middle of a grade three rapid unable to free myself, going nowhere. Fortunately, help was at hand (Subsequently my dog's tail now is removed from my kayak).

A friend of mine, Gareth has similar stories. We were paddling the Wye from Builth Wells to Glasbury. Not a difficult section of the river. But when it came to Hell Hole, the water level being low, a tricky S-bend in the flow had to be negotiated. Gareth unfortunately capsized and was momentarily held in the confused water. He bailed out. The rescue was easy, but where was his paddle? We looked everywhere before concluding that it must still be in the hole, but how?

On the river Coruh in Turkey, after the end of our third day, paddling in the relatively easy water, we approached the town of Ispir. We planned to camp just below the town. This meant negotiating a grade 4 rapid. The waves were rather large and confused in places. Somewhere in the middle, Gareth capsized and failed to roll. It was about 4:00 p.m. The following morning, at about 8:00 a.m., Gareth's brother Chris went down to the river. As he was performing the usual morning activities he spotted the lost paddles, The metal edge of the blades had crimped up and was lightly resting on the top of a boulder in the swiftly flowing river and must have been there all night after getting delayed in the rapids above. It had done 4 km stayed overnight and became stuck just where we camped.

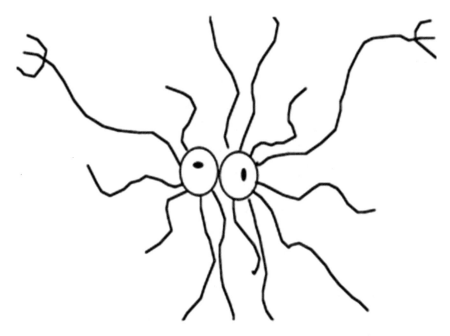

Impression of a Scrimbly. Drawn by Steven Lawrence (Loz) after a close encounter, when trapped under a boulder in Troutal gorge on the River Duddon

So did the branch happen by accident or was it placed there, did the spike of rock suddenly grow or were the others just lucky? Can pieces of tape knot themselves around trees? Does Hell Hole eat paddles or was something holding the paddle down? Could a paddle spend 14 hours perched on a rock in a surging grade 2 rapid or were the Scrimblies just being kind?

If you think about it Scrimbly activity can happen anywhere but most often it happens to novices, or on more difficult rapids and rivers. Is this just chance or is it the work of the Scrimblies?

Further research on the occurrence of incidents involving Scrimblies has led to several theories as to their existence and habits.

In rivers that flow through deep gorges, more incidents seem to occur. It is therefore presumed that these Scrimblies that inhabit such places are older and more experienced. In these gorges, Scrimblies mature and learn their trade. It has been noted that there are often unusual rock formations in the shape of holes and small caves. Perhaps in these formations, the Scrimblies breed.

When hatched, the Scrimbly may serve an apprenticeship as a Squiggly. The apprenticeship is done in tree-lined rivers where twigs and branches protrude from the river bed. Squiggly gets hold of the tree parts and irregularly moves them around trying to frighten off paddlers. Some Squigglys never seem to graduate and so, as they grow, they move onto larger branches and even trees, which they drag in rivers when the river is in spate.

After learning to scare paddlers, Scrimblies need to get some real experience; so wait for novice paddlers. In easy rapids, they lurk, hone their skills, coordinate the thrusts of their actions and learn to perfect the timing of their attacks. After a capsize the more mischievous type learns to untie all the kit from the inside of your boat. so that it all floats off in different directions. More experienced paddlers will not be affected by the inexperienced Scrimblies and so pass unhindered. However, mature Scrimblies will even attack the most expert paddlers, displacing them onto rocks, and causing great embarrassment. The fully-fledged Scrimbly lurks in more difficult rapids and pools to finely tune their skills. Some are good at sucking boats down, others rely on pushing boats onto rocks or under overhangs. They blow-up boils of water to deflect the kayak onto undercut rocks and boulders. The more sophisticated Scrimbly will attack at the last moment, just pushing the boat from its intended course giving its occupant no time to correct their error. More violent types have perfected the act of causing capsizes and even grabbing the stern of a kayak and dragging it down, thus disorientating the paddler into a back loop. The Scrimbly then pulls at the paddle so that it is usually quite difficult to roll up quickly after such a manoeuvre.

Scrimblies are generally playful things, doing their business for a laugh without intent or malice. They do this because, as with all living things, they need to feed. Scrimblies feed on the echoes of a paddler's ego and are ever hungry.

Can you see a Scrimbly?

The bigger the paddler's ego is, the bigger the meal. The cocky and the over-confident are the most attractive victims for the Scrimbly as to get one of these to swim can result in a super-size dinner. Scrimblies are most agitated after long periods of dry weather when they get very hungry, and the out-of-practice paddler attempts those rapids and falls that should be easy but...

A Scrimbly at work

There are two schools of thought about the origins of Scrimblies. The 'location theory' and the 'life theory'. The more popular location theory is that

Scrimblies tend to live in one place, they stay at the same rapid or fall all the time and perfect their fun. They become experts at causing havoc at a particular spot and so many paddlers will be seen to have similar problems or capsize in the same way time after time. At a good spot, the Scrimbly will be well-fed. Some falls and rapids do not have a guardian Scrimbly and so do not cause any problems for paddlers. Perhaps there are a few that service a number of rapids and so paddlers have problems on a drop one day, but on a different fall the next time they paddle the river.

The less popular 'Life theory' proposes that when you are born, your own Scrimbly is born at the same time. As you grow up your Scrimbly does also. If you start to paddle when you are young, your Scrimbly will be less experienced. Maybe only a Squiggly and so you may never have many Scrimbly problems. If you wait until you are older, your Scrimbly will be very experienced, more so than you, so you will have many problems whilst learning to paddle. If you paddle on a river, your Scrimbly may be there and get you. But if soon after you paddle in a different river system you may be lucky as your Scrimbly will have to go all the way to the sea and back up the new river in order to get you. You may be able to fool it by not deciding which river to paddle, until the last minute. If you are a good paddler then your Scrimbly may never get you properly and it may develop into a gorge monster so that when it does get you it will be serious for you. Of course, some Scrimblies are meaner and fall outside the Scrimbly code of ethics. These mean ones have developed their own subculture and their only desire is to hurt and injure the paddler. These are the gorge monsters. They hold you in holes until you can't breathe. They look out for loose lines to ensnare on rocks and drag you to the river bed. They capsize you onto rocks to cut your face and twist your paddle to dislocate your shoulder. The real extreme gorge monsters will do their utmost to make you swim a nasty rapid and they have been known to kill.

You have all paddled rapids and we have all portaged rapids. Why? Perhaps it is because the Scrimblies are working away at our subconscious making us unsure. Perhaps we can subliminally sense the presence of Scrimblies and gorge monsters and prefer not to do battle with them. Finally, there are two more groups of paddlers, those who seek out the gorge monsters and relish the fight, they are becoming more common. They seek out new rapids and falls and get them done before the Scrimblies appear. Then there are those paddlers who don't believe...

Scrimblies

Scrimblies are sung on a tape by the Stranglers
Who thought they might be twisted-up anglers?
But no. They have more devious ways
Of ruining your sport on cold winter days
They shimmer and wave in the shade of the sun
And surf frothy waves to the annoyance of some.
Playful or churlish, so changes their mood,
Unusually dangerous and always quite rude

They hide in the roots of trees on the bank
In slimy, dark crevices, dingy and dank
Under boulders, they slink slither and slide
Frequently there, but can never be spied.
Are they thin, are they fat, short, ugly or tall?
A gurgling roar, of their unhearable call.
They blend with the river, rocks and the sea.
So seeing a Scrimbly is quite beyond me.

Well what are these Scrimblies, what do they do?
Besides hiding out of sight of me and of you.
They cause all the problems that we have on rivers.
Think about it! You may get the shivers.
When rivers in spate emergent twigs, we call wiggly
But really it's the work of a form called a Squiggly.
A Scrimbly eats ego, gorge monsters our souls
Both generally live as underwater moles.

Scrimblies are fun, playful devils indeed,
Holding your paddle in your hour of need.
Always you'll float straight towards branches
Or get stuck on rocks when little the chance is.
At the bottom of falls that look clear and deep
Scrimblies surprise you with half-rotten sheep
It's always a surprise, but fall in you will
Despite oodles of training, technique and skill.

After capsizing your boat, it will stay on its side
Under the guidance of those scrimbly eyes.
They make tricky your attempt at an Eskimo roll
Since your swim and embarrassment are their ultimate goal.
The one thing about Scrimblies is they always strike
On your left side, because you're looking right.
'Cos Scrimblies will get you. That is their game
Though seemingly senseless and always inane.

So where do they come from these terrible foes?
They grow into gorge monsters everyone knows.
From holes in a cliff, they fall into the stream
And develop habits that can be obscene.
So you better watch out. You'd better take care
The Scrimblies are waiting, they're always there.
Be it flat, be it foaming or even in spate
The Scrimblies will get paddlers. You are the bait!

Poem by the author

Dourbie or not Dourbie

It proved to be a big test of all I knew.
(April 1989)

Richard Evans, Piers Nesbitt, Chris Walker, Colin Unwin

Dourbie or not Dourbie? That is the question we were asking ourselves. We sat in the bar of a French hotel just north of Florac, Central Massif, France. The conversation had been about the thrills, adrenaline rushes and swims on the lemming descent of the upper Tarn gorge two days earlier. The previous day we had driven to the river Trevezel, a limestone gorge river, only to find no water. We had carried on to the upper Dourbie, which was low but paddleable. The granite bedrock was similar to that on the upper Tarn, which was promised for a challenging paddle. The river level gauge is to be found 300 m downstream (at an old bridge), from the road bridge at Prunaret. Our German guidebook suggested 80 cm to be the best level. After a scramble through some bushes and a climb down some rocks, we saw the gauge reading at 65 cm. It would be scrapey. The guide hinted grade at 3-4 with three portages for the upper section. Since it was now early afternoon, most decided to give it a miss but Colin Unwin and Richard Evans and I were keen for some fun. The river proved to be 4-5 with six portages. Shallow bouldery rapids soon led to clean bedrock and large boulders and some beautiful falls and rapids. The 4 km run took the three of us 2 hours to complete.

So that evening with the buzz of the upper Dourbie still in our veins we were trying to persuade some of the others to join us on a trip down the main gorge of the Dourbie. Various points of view were expressed, but despite the excess wine, only Piers and Chris decided to take the plunge and join us.

The information we had managed to translate from our German DKV guidebook went as follows:

'The Dourbie is a typical river of the region, with its gorges, falls and steep gradient (for comparison 'it is more difficult than the Tarn gorge or the Veccio (in Corsica). Dourbie Bridge to Le Taynac 5 and 6, 8 km. Le Taynac to St. Jean to Bruel 3 and 4, 4 km. Dourbie Bridge, the start of the 'Great Gorges of the Dourbie' This is a most impressive gorge having extreme difficulties of white-water grade 5 and 6 Up to 15 portages which are exhausting. Ropes are essential. It is not possible to get out of the gorge. The river rises quickly in rain and becomes impassable. =The most favourable water is when it is just possible to canoe on the river at the 'bridge at Dourbie' allow 8–12 hours.'

This last sentence got us worried since the water at the put-in bridge was deep. However, the weather was settled, we estimated 8 hours for the trip so we decided on an early start the next morning.

Chris was up at 7:00 a.m. from a frustrated sleep of fitful dreams about possible ensuing dramas. He noted 'something inside me is disturbed' and not perhaps unreasonably. He lay there, wondering what was ahead, having already 'repaddled' in his head, the previous day's events on the Tarn. Feeling the effects of the previous night's indulgences, a light breakfast saw five of us set off at 8:30 a.m., to the Dourbie. The drive from Florac to Dourbie took about 1.5 hours, so we arrived at Dourbie bridge rather later than we had planned. To save time we agreed that Chris and I would do the shuttle and try to get some idea of the river gorge while the other three set off, agreeing to meet at the first difficult fall which they would look at and wait for us.

The drive showed us a boulder-blocked grade 4 section a few hundred metres from the bridge, then the river disappeared into the trees. The D114 was a narrow winding road and climbed slowly, twisting through small villages. The river was not visible. Part of the way down we could see there were two large loops and on one of them about 800m below, we could see a section of waterfall, flat, fall, flat, fall series for about 500 m. We were unable to find the egress, a footbridge at Le Taynac (*a lane leads from the D114 to Le Taynac, and from there a 10-minute walk leads to the river*) and so we were forced to continue a few more kilometres to just above the town of Le Viala where we met some Germans. They had spent 12 hours in the gorge the day before and had to leave their boats when it got dark and walk 3 km along the riverbank. I remarked to Chris, '*Better not to tell the others.*'

By the time Chris and I returned to the bridge at Dourbie, the others had gone, so we were obliged to follow. We reached the boulder field that we had previously seen from the road. Not too difficult, but one drop needed inspecting. I got out, to see Chris drop between two 5m rounded granite boulders, only to leave his paddle jammed between them. He headed for the next 2 m drop that I'd just got out to inspect. I threw my left-handed paddle to right-handed Chris, which he caught. His potential for capsizing with a wrong-handed paddle was increased. Chris frantically back-paddled and managed to stop himself before going over the drop.

His paddle retrieved, we continued on grade 3 rapids with the odd fall. Constant concentration was needed to find the deeper water which was crystal clear. Twenty minutes later we hadn't seen the others but our confidence grew as our muscles warmed we thought that the river couldn't be that hard or they would have waited.

A few minutes later, my heart started pumping harder as we saw them waiting on the right bank. PFE no doubt. The rapid they had stopped at was the first event horizon, where the river fell from sight. The inspection set us whooping at the clean bedrock with crystal clear water. Two small falls followed by a 1 m drop into a narrow channel, the left of which was overhung by a 3 m rounded boulder.

The first sequence of falls into the gorge

The boil underneath this boulder was no place to be, so an angled approach, aiming left was needed. This was followed by a beautiful slide about 3 m long with several bubbly cushions. I volunteered to be the probe, followed by Richard and Colin. When Chris came down he again jammed his paddle between the overhanging boulder and the bedrock and slid down the slide without his paddle. Fortunately, going straight through the boiling stopper at the bottom.

Another 20 m saw another inspection. A 2 m+ fall into a tight pool, then another 2 m with a difficult overhanging boulder on the right.

The technique here was to paddle the nose of the boat as far onto the steep rock on the left as possible and slide down to avoid the worst of the overhang. Again I went first. The water on the lip of the chute looked green and solid, but as I passed over it I sank deep into the aerated water. My paddle curved, braced on the boulders as I sank into the fall. Fearing it would snap, I let go, my paddle recoiled about 3 m into the air, (which is all those at the top saw) and luckily landed beside me in the downstream pool. The 2nd drop was wider. Chris followed, sank in the aerated water and capsized next to the boulder but rolled up in time for the bottom drop.

Richard negotiates the tricky boulder drop

Similar rapids and falls followed in quick succession. The next difficult fall consisted of a 1 m drop into a pool, a 1.2 m fall with a bit of an overhang, and then a 90° left turn to fall 1.5m into 'aero'. Colin in his Rotobat disappeared completely, to emerge a few seconds later as the buoyancy sent him flying completely out of the water. He settled just in time to go over the final drop in reverse before capsizing and swimming out to safety. As the sun shone brightly, the river became even more choked with boulders. However, we were confident that our skills and experience would be sufficient to deal with the problems the river would throw at us.

Colin going aero

Our next problem came when an inspection was carried out from a cliff 5 m above the drop. This, of course, gave us a false perspective, but there was no choice. The best route seemed to go right, slide 1 m, turn 90° to the left, drop 3 m, turn 90° to the right, drop 2 m and run out between boulders.

Again I was a probe. A small stopper above me pushed me to the left, an MOT. I took the whole 4 m in one go, being deflected left into a cave hidden under a boulder, which we had not seen. Fortunately, I was able to back out easily and line up for the final 2 m drop.

Then came Chris in his Dancer. On the 1 m drop, he stopped dead, not pinned, but his boat bobbed up and down as it held its 45° angle on the fall. His bow had become trapped under a rock. Thankfully Chris was in no immediate danger. Scrambling back up the smooth granite to get above Chris, I threw him a line from upstream. He wrapped the rope around his hand and pulled. The upstream pull worked, and he came free. but his bow shot forward. His stern was taken by the current and he went off the 3 m drop backwards rope in hand. He popped back up vertically and I saw the bow of the boat reappear at the top of the fall. As gravity took over again Chris managed to support himself with his paddle to prevent a capsize as he fell back into the pool. He untangled the rope and took the final drop in this section very shaken.

A typical complex drop. Piers finding a way through

We were being tested, continuously not far from our limit.

More falls followed, all of which needed inspection. We'd made less than 1 km in the last hour and clearly, this gorge was going to take a very long time. We decided to change tactics. As soon as two of us were free at the bottom of a fall they would go ahead and decide the line on the next fall. This of course meant that you had to paddle the fall/drop/slide on someone else's say-so, but more speed was required. The next serious problem was a small drop onto a bedrock slide, which passed behind the then through a 4 m waterfall. We called it the 'Curtain' and portaged it. This was followed by a beautiful fall of 4 m, with only one problem, a boulder protruding in the middle, from which all the water deflected left or right into small cliffs, portage again. It may have gone but being in this gorge, caution was needed: we couldn't afford any disasters.

Next, an impressive 5 m waterfall onto boulders and another portage. The Dourbie was proving a hard nut to crack, causing more incidents than we had bargained for. After a 100 m flat pool, we were forced to do another portage past a steep, fast-flowing rift blocked by boulders. As Richard moved across the steep slabs above he slipped and, in the process of trying to prevent himself from sliding into the nastiness below, he let go of his Spud kayak. It fell into the rift. We were contemplating how we might retrieve it. Instead of getting stuck, it bounced between boulders and shot off across the pool and over the next fall. We were fortunate since I had almost completed the portage. So after sliding over the fall, I caught the spud as it slowly drifted across the next flat pool. "If you don't want to paddle the river you just have to say so," we joked with Richard.

Looking back upstream, we were amazed at the steepness of the section we had just completed. Falls stacked one on top of the other. What a river! already a big adventure and we weren't even halfway down. This was the stuff of nightmares or dreams depending on your perspective. For Chris, it was erring towards the latter, his MOT status growing with every drop. The rest of us yearned to see what challenge awaited us just around just the next corner.

Time was getting on and the blue sky was clouding over. The difficulties eased for a while, we found mainly class 2–3 boulder fields, often shallow. The relief from the ever-present dangers was evident on everyone's face. Paddling a deep inaccessible gorge is worth it, even if the water is slowly flowing. Fill it with a never-ending cavalcade of big slabs, narrow chutes and combination drops and you have a wild water dream. We were in this dream.

Richard takes the Slab slide

We then came to some slabs, an easily angled rocky slide 8 m long. Followed by a pool to regain your thoughts. Then a steeper 10 m long slab, guarded by cliffs on either side. From the top of the first fall, you could not see the bottom of the second and yet having slid down the first slide there was no way out. It proved to be a classic, horizontal at the top to vertical at the bottom, so convex shaped, falling about 6 m in total.

Again the steep-sided gorge relented and more shallow boulder mazes followed. Things were getting easier. Perhaps we had done more than we thought. Soon the shallow section became tedious as the river was wider, so we often became stuck on boulders just under the surface. So with some trepidation, we were pleased to see the gorge narrow again after 400 m.

The rapids were now class 4, but the water was deep, and we were able to work out the route from our kayaks and paddle on sight until we came across a 3 m wide slot. I got out to inspect.

Tow back in the narrow slot sucks the rear end of the kayak down

A plank spanned the slot where a 1.5 m drop fell into FWD where a holding stopper, led to bubbleosity (water full of bubbles where it would be hard to get the full force of a paddle stroke, as the percentage of air in the water was great.) I figured a fast approach was required, with a boof to clear the stopper, followed by deep paddle strokes, to maybe find sufficient water to gain enough purchase to thrust the kayak forward.

Passing this information to the others I stood with my safety line and watched Piers, Colin and Richard through with no problem. I figured Chris would be OK so I went back to my boat to take my turn. Just as I did this, Chris took the drop, capsized, dislocated his shoulder and swam. The tow back from the stopper made it difficult for him to swim out, so my throw line was deployed into action. The stopper held his Dancer for even longer.

I shot the fall and in the process of capsizing, I perfectly jammed my 208 cm Schlegl paddles into the 208 cm gap between the walls. I did a hand roll but was pulled back towards the stopper until the jammed paddle stopped me. A sharp pull on the paddle released it and I was able to escape without further problems. Which is more than can be said for Chris. Downstream from 'Dancer's folly', Chris was in some pain from his shoulder which he had dislocated prior to this trip. Given his injury and loss of confidence, he did not wish to continue. But Hobson presented the only choice. To carry on.

I was a bit surprised when I looked at my watch to see it was 3:00 p.m. Despite the time, we took the opportunity to stop, rest, and take on a morsel of food, absorb our situation, consider the options and let Chris recover a little. We had eaten nothing since breakfast. A tin of rice pudding and 100 g of cheese do not go far between five hungry paddlers in a deep gorge.

Our choices; paddle on, going back upstream would take hours, getting to the road almost 600 m above the south side of the steep wooded gorge. The north side is even steeper and higher. All seemed impossible even if you could find your way past the lines of broken cliffs. The commitment you make when entering a big river gorge had caught up with us. There was only one option, wincing in anticipation of a different sort of MOT, Chris pushed his chest forward and shoulder back so that his shoulder popped back in.

The next section was, fortunately, easier, even scrapey, as the river bed was wider, the water more spread out, but still pleasant to paddle and even allowed a chance to relax, a short break from the demands of what we had already descended.

Maybe it lasted 600 m, until an awkward narrow chute between two boulders in the middle of the river. Richard inspected and gave us the thumbs up. Sometimes luck plays its part. The first two came through from the left and angled right and slid through with no problem.

Richard takes the gap between the boulders that trapped Chris but heading right and in a shorter kayak – he had no problem.

Chris approached from the right, glanced off a submerged boulder and stopped dead in the chute between the boulders. Pinned by an underwater rock, he sank in the fall as water piled up behind him until just his head stuck out. This was serious. By the time he had stopped slowly sinking, we had seen the danger and were all out on the left bank. Richard's accurate first-time throw of his safety rope landed in Chris's hand, 5 m away in the middle of the river. It is good to know that time spent practising really helps. The rope did not help but it was obvious the immediate danger was over as Chris had stopped sinking and he could breathe - just.

Colin and I waded into the river. Meanwhile, Chris had managed to reach back to a tape he had tied onto the rear of his boat, just for such an occasion. He pulled his spray deck free and tried to pull himself out.

The danger now became the force of the water, pushing him forward as his thighs became free, possibly snapping his legs at the knee.

Understandably stressed, Chris was not up for waiting for help to get to him, so pulling backwards on the tape he freed one leg, but was unable to get his other leg free. Colin and I had now crossed the river. A scream erupted as his leg was forced onto the cockpit rim. He held his own against the water for about a minute. By repositioning his backside on the cockpit he managed to change the direction of the force of the water and crawl out just as we reached him.

Two boulders that finally tipped the balance for Chris. You might just see the tip of a yellow kayak underwater between the boulders.

Richard helped Chris to the bank whilst Colin and I contrived to clip a rope to the rear end of the Dancer, From the bank, Piers and Richard pulled it free.

Chris's dancer was in a bad way, half-folded and twisted, but still in one piece and with no holes. Its owner was not feeling so good either.

Chris compares his feelings now with those of the upper Tarn gorges 2 days before

'*The quality of the water and the paddling awakened a previously untapped excitement in my paddling without fear, a sensation of pure enjoyment.*

Yet here, continuous adrenaline rushes followed by a series of mistakes and misadventures ate away at the enjoyment, played on my fear and which for me, became a survival epic. I now became aware that I was out of my depth. The water even at this low level, still plays powerfully on my boat. What would the river be like with an extra foot more water? Only the devil knows.'

Chris had decided he was too close to passing his line of misadventure.

As discussed earlier, the only realistic option is to carry on downstream. We hoped the heat of the sun might help to return Chris's bent kayak to a better shape, but the clouds rolled in. However, Chris had had enough and we were forced to contemplate what we had previously thought was not possible: to walk out of the gorge. He was adamant he was not paddling anymore, he was walking out. But where? There was no path. The sides were very steep, dotted with cliffs and scree slopes but also covered with trees, so you could not pick out a way to go. Chris was not for being swayed. He was not intending to paddle another metre. After some discussion, a plan emerged. Piers volunteered to go with Chris. They agreed to carry their boats down the south riverbank until they could find an easy way up to the road.

With some apprehension, we left them to find their way up to the road and paddled off, wondering when we would see them again.

Back to inspecting each drop in the river. One very bouldery section of about 80 m needed portaging over the rocks in the middle of the river, as high cliffs lined both banks. In high water, this would be impossible, so paddling it would be the only option. Flat water below, we followed cliffs which led us around a right-angled corner as the river changed direction.

Then it struck me, this could be the section I had seen from the road. Or maybe it wasn't. I mentioned this to Richard and Colin, and we looked up and thought we could imagine a line of the road or were we just seeing things? If it were true, it was only a kilometre to the egress point that we could not find from the road earlier in the day. We decided to go back to where we had left Piers and Chris and help them as it would be possible to carry the boats out downstream. One kilometre upstream, 20 minutes later, we were back where we left them but no sign. We looked up and saw a yellow kayak on a small ridge about 200m up, but still no sign of our friends.

We returned to the mission. The next fall looked easy enough from above, or so I thought. *Pick up some speed, aim hard left, hit the cushion of water on the wall, turn right, and slide 3 m down a slab into the pool below.*

I was surprised when Colin paddled straight onto the ramp so avoiding the cushion. He hit the ramp hard but made it OK.

Richard went the way we had planned but a surprising boil above the ramp pushed him right and he disappeared under the waterfall to emerge a few seconds later in the pool below.

Richard emerges from beneath the fall below where I stood!

Suddenly it seemed a whole lot more difficult. Sometimes being probe is easier on the mind. The slab was not flat but angled. I followed my planned route, *I paddled as hard as I could to rise over the cushion. It made no difference; I followed the same route as Richard. As I went under the fall I dropped into a narrow slot and stopped. Time for a lump in the throat.*

MOT an 'oh my god' thought. Then forward momentum, the rocks scraped both sides of my kayak, and then my buoyancy aid before the force of the water pushed me through. A lucky escape. Had I been fatter or my kayak wider, the outcome could have been so different.

With difficulty, we inspected the next horror show, a 4 m vertical drop into a shallow still pool, with an awkward lip, so no possibility of landing flat. The worst scenario could be to pin the kayak or break your ankles. What a choice. After a bit of hunting, we noticed a few small ledges, and we reckoned on lowering the boats into the pool and climbing down afterwards.

Meanwhile, back up the gorge, the river bank proved too arduous and so Chris and Piers decided to go straight up. Chris continues *'The hot sunshine had now returned and after only 50 m we were sweating and gasping for air. We were soon peeled down to our thermals. We discovered it easier to carry one boat between two and then come back for the second boat. This meant twice the distance, twice the climbing, and twice the height. We thought of making it easier by clipping a sling to each end of the kayak and carrying the boat over our shoulders.'*

Meanwhile back at the river, the flat sections between falls became longer. The drops themselves became easier. The gorge opened out and the drops became rapids. It had taken about 6 hours to cover 6 km of the river.

Then a new hazard.; willow trees lined the banks so that the correct route choice became more difficult to see. However, our progress increased, and with no more portages to slow us, we covered 2 km in about half an hour. A small bridge crossed the river. This must be Le Taynac with a narrow leafy track leading to it from the road above.

Grinning at each other and then smiling with joy, the relief of escaping the gorge was shared by the three of us. Our thoughts soon turned to Chris and Piers, where were they? Were they safe? Were they still in the gorge?

Chris continues *'Two hours later, after much contouring and vertical gain, we reached a clearing and then a track. We left the boats at the clearing, and after a further 30 minutes the track leads to the road.'*

Our spirits were high but, as Chris and I had been unable to find the Le Taynac egress early in the day, we still had 4 km of class 3/4 river to negotiate before we reached my car. The next 2 km took an hour. The whole section was generally easier but still required three inspections and ended with a weir. We portaged the weir and rounded the next corner to see a man waving at us. He was an Italian paddler who immediately offered us a lift to our car. We wanted to complete the river as planned, but by now we were quite chilled having spent over 7 hours on the river. It was getting dark and finding the others was paramount so we gladly accepted. The forest track emerged on the road on a hidden bend which explained why we had not seen it in the morning when we did the shuttle with the cars.

Having been dropped at our car 2 km further downstream, we rushed back up the winding D114.

Meanwhile Chris and Piers further up the valley. '*We chatted about the events of the day as we walked down the road hoping to meet the others sooner rather than later. Six kilometres later, it was getting dark when the Renault appeared and we were found*'.

As we rounded each corner searching for signs of Chris and Piers we became more and more worried. Then, 6 km, later, we rounded a corner and were elated to see them. There were hugs all around as we squashed all five of us into the car.

Ninety minutes later, we had retrieved their boats from 100m down a track, and then the other car from the start of our trip, before marching into the local hotel and asked for a table for five. We looked bedraggled. The waiter looked at us, shrugging his shoulders. We told him we had just paddled the gorge. So he led us into the basement away from the other diners. It was an hour, a gallon of water and five baskets of bread later before we finally got a table for dinner.

So the guidebook should read "*Dourbie Bridge, the start of the 'Great Gorges of the Dourbie'.*

This is a most impressive gorge having extreme difficulties of white-water grade 5 and 6. Six portages at least. An exhausting trip with extended hard sections. Ropes are essential. All falls can be portaged except one in high water. It is possible to get out of the gorge with difficulty. The river rises quickly in rain and becomes impassable. The most favourable water is when it is just possible to kayak on the river at the 'bridge at Punaret, 80 cm on the gauge."

That night, too tired to erect tents, we bivvied out in a campsite. My mind thought about how we might have had a different outcome. I recalled those endless sweet lines, again and again, and considered the choices we had made, giggling to myself until my thoughts merged with dreams.

Elverpaddling

Norway (July 1989)

Pip Line, Sten Sture, Angela Sture, Richard Evans

I don't recall whose idea it was to go to Norway. Sten and Angela Sture took their car, Pip Line and myself in another car, with Richard Evans travelling in whichever car he liked. This proved to be a good arrangement; since both Pip and Angela would happily paddle grade 3 and cope with grade 4, but weren't so keen about paddling harder rivers. This meant that when the lads were off doing the business, the lasses could paddle something easier or amuse themselves after leaving a car at our egress point.

Taking into consideration the cost of food in Norway, our trip planning was a bit more involved than the usual trip to the Alps. We decided to take all our food with us, allocating several days to each person who would be responsible for providing the meals for the group.

We were late meeting the Stures at Kirkby Stephen and had to drive like lunatics to Newcastle, where the ferry operator wouldn't let us on the ferry unless we took the kayaks off the car roofs. After paying £10 for the marvellous eat-all-you-can smorgasbord buffet, Sten felt the effects of a lumpy sea, which meant he couldn't enjoy more than a bowl of soup. Our journey was slightly delayed at Bergen, as Richard had to ring up for his A-level results, which came out on the day that we left. Although we thought they were a great set of results Richard seemed to be mumbling about Geography. Soon open roads, wild scenes and waterfalls in spate caught our imagination, as we excitedly anticipated the adventures to come. Several hours, two ferries later we arrived at the Jostedalselva. Camping was our intention, but heavy rain put us off. Those who have travelled to Norway will know about the 'hytte', which cost about £5 a night each at the time. We could not resist a warm dry hut with a cooker and bunk beds.

Jostedalselva. Driving up the road by the Jostedalselva to Gjerde, our eyes were taken by the size of the river. Every time we stopped by a road tunnel there seemed to be a horror show of white frothiness, FWD, big and powerful with enormous stoppers. This was puzzling since our guidebook- 'Elverpaddling' didn't prepare us for what we saw.

Typical section one of the Jostadelva gorges

The gauge by the road to Vigdal read 1.7 m below the top, but we had no idea of what this meant in terms of comparative water levels. Although it looked a bit pushy, there were going to be several portages, but this wasn't going to be one of those ultra-committing trips as the road ran next to the river. Richard, Sten and I braved the drizzle and set off, happy with the option of being able to egress to the road at any time. Easy water at first, allowed us to become accustomed to the speed of the water, but not to its temperature, as it flowed from a glacier only a few kilometres upstream.

Sten entering the first gorge

Grade 3 rapids seemed to suffice to get our arms back into the swing of things, or so we thought, until entering a class 4 drop at the first of several small gorges.

At the end of this gorge, the water got a bit meaner. Looking back over my shoulder, I noticed a yellow boat dropping into a hole that I couldn't see into.

What was he doing? Come on, Sten; roll. The flow washed the upturned boat free of the stopper but under the overhanging cliffs on the left. Here we go! Our first swim as Richard and I prepared for the rescue. But no, Sten fooled us both by rolling up. Unfortunately, it is so hard to roll against the cushion on a cliff, and so as his head came free, the boat reverted to its upturned state. Luck favours the valiant and his efforts had freed him from the undercuts and so he rolled again, successfully this time. Although numbed by the water, Sten was beaming, very pleased with himself. We were certainly well impressed.

We floated downstream on easier water until the start of the second gorge. The second gorge held a river-wide stopper at its downstream end.

Sten Sten finally escapes the hole

Once committed... Richard and I found an easy enough route through the guarding hole. As Sten followed our route exactly, a wave loomed up. This forced him sideways to allow him to give us another fine display of back loop, roll, front loop, roll, over again, roll at the third attempt, after washing from the hole. Who was playing with whom we wondered? We had to be impressed with his tenacity in hanging in there.

Terribly cold now and a bit shaken, Sten braved a few more kilometres before deciding to get off.

Beside a road tunnel, a class 5-6 run, over ledges for a big but messy 200m, found us portaging. At the second tunnel, an inspection of what we dubbed 'Tigger Gorge' (the wonderful thing about Tiggers is... they go bouncy, bouncy...), one of the waves momentarily and unpredictably grew up to about 4m, shaped like a pyramid and nearly vertical at the top before breaking like classic surf on a good day.

Paddling up that monster wave I feel the adrenaline pumping until I crest and plunged down the far side, I gain support by bracing my paddle on the waves that followed. Now Tiggers are wonderful things. Two more portages at tunnels were followed by long and continuous grade 4 water with many holes to be avoided. Superb paddling, especially when a pour-over grabbed my back end and I spent the next 50 m pointing skywards, fighting to get control back. Twenty-six kilometres of the river took us 7 hours with the portaging and a stop for lunch. We had been a little surprised by the volume of the water and its cold temperature, but equally impressed with how we coped. The evening was idled away with the chatter of things to come.

On our return journey, we passed the Jostadelva. It was some 2 m lower. What we hadn't realised is that it had rained for three days solidly just before we got to Norway.

Richard on a Sjoa play wave

Sjoa The following day, Richard and I carried our boats 1 km to the Sjoa at Ridderspranget. Seal launching into the gorge was perhaps foolish, but once you are in you're in. Swift flowing grade 4 with some 5 for 500 m brought us to easier water and we drifted to the bridge at Brurusti where the others joined us as we portaged around some rather long impressive slabs, each terminating in a river-wide stopper. Another seal launch seemed to be the easiest way to shorten the portage.

Richard Evans on play wave Sjoa

Yet another portage, this time around Nedre Trasafoss, led to some fine water and scenery interspersed with more mellow stretches. The gorge in this section is virtually inescapable and at 8 km, a big commitment and equally big challenge, just harder than grade 4 but never quite 5. There were many large pour-overs to avoid and careful route choice was needed, contributing to a classic piece of paddling. Two days later, we found ourselves on another section of the Sjoa. A classic in many senses of the word, with something for everyone. Nine kilometres in four hours with plenty of play waves. Underneath the road bridge at Kruke, a stopper provides an excellent site for photographs from above.

That night, just as we were going to bed, someone went out for a pee '*what are those funny lights in the sky.*' We all jumped out of our sleeping bags and drove for 20 minutes to the top of the nearest hill, where we sat agog for two hours as the light of the Aurora pulsed ever-variable patterns, green and yellow across the sky.

Frya Being used to paddling in the Lake District with its small rocky becks, The bigger volume of water, with no rocks that we found so far, wasn't our usual scene. We fancied something rockier! We scoured the guidebook and nearby was the Frya which became our next target. After looking at our road map of Europe, the less than helpful comment in the guidebook stated maps are essential to finding suitable pull-out places. Saeter is a suitable place, but where is it? Saeter turned out to be three houses by the road and a cart track that ended in a field 200 m above the edge of the box-like canyon. Not on our road map.

Sten just entering the Frya gorge

Some 15 m below we noticed a small cairn and decided that must be it, although the way up the cliffs was far from obvious. Driving upstream, the road past Hovde cost us Kr. 20 toll, then brought us to a small bridge over the river. Angela decided this was not for her. A sensible decision as things turned out.

Soon after setting off, we entered the gorge and the shallow shingly rapids seemed to indicate that the water was low, thus telling us that Angela had made the best decision. Going back wasn't an option.

Fortunately, the shingle gave way to sandstone and shale bedrock so the river narrowed so becoming deeper, thus more paddleable.

Twisty gorge

The constantly twisting gorge meandered with the sides growing and shrinking as we cruised down the pleasant class 3 rapids. However, with its box-like nature and the constant wonder of what's just around the next corner, we were always wary. It always felt like PFE, constantly needing to be ready to power into that next eddy and get out to inspect. Time and kilometres passed without incident even though there was one harder section of more continuous small drops.

After what seemed ages, but was probably 2 hours, we drifted past the cairn almost missing it. Here we helped Pip to escape up an obvious if rather a steep gully. The guidebook mentioned that after this point the river became more difficult.

As the guidebook suggested, the gradient increased noticeably and the width narrowed down to 2m in places. The bends in the gorge became more contorted.

The drops were higher; some of which needed inspecting. A few of these proved quite awkward to asses the route and then follow it. However, we made good progress.

Always wary, by alternating in spotting lines and directing each other through we progressed quickly, but without taking undue risks.

A typical Frya gorge drop

Sten on line

After a wider section, where the rocks seemed very jagged, and the sides became overhanging schist, my MOT built. More inspections were needed as the river narrowed even more. We found a rhythm, we slowly became accustomed to the nature of this bedrock, schist river. We gained confidence, paddling more freely, as we learned the river's nature. Or so we thought.

I found myself pressed against the cliff, on river left, straining to try to see over the next drop. '*What did the guidebook say about this bit?*'

'*Some terminal waterfalls, I think,*' came the reply. '*Yes an easier section followed by some terminal falls, but we should have got out before we reach them.*' In the narrow gorge, the previous section had been easier, but no obvious get out had been seen in the small cliffs that line either bank. 'Better get out and have a look.'

Having paddled our boats onto the small shingle bank on the opposite side of the river, we hopped out. I still could not see over the fall. Richard edged along a narrowing ledge '*What does it look like?*' I inquired. '*The fall is ledges and about 3 m in all but I can't see the bottom or around the* corner.' came the reply. Pointing across the river, we both noticed a small eddy on the opposite side just above the fall. From there we should be able to see around the corner.

At that moment, Sten caught us up. '*It's probably OK, don't suppose you fancy paddling to the other side for a look*'. Seeing the flow rate and vertical cliff of the far bank '*How do I get back if I don't like what I see*', came the reply. '*Ah, we'll attach a throw line to help you.*' and *pull you back if you can't paddle; it's only a few metres.*' Reassured he decided to try. Unfortunately, at water level, from that eddy Sten couldn't see any more than us. He tried to paddle back upstream but the flow was faster than it looked. Throw line delivered, Sten attached it to his quick-release harness on his buoyancy aid. He tried again. This time we pulled, but the water was too swift. MOT for us all. The river won, and the undesirable became the actuality. Sten turned to do a blind descent. No point holding onto this I thought, as Sten went out of sight. I let the rope run out between my fingers, following him. I couldn't believe it, What idiots we were, he was gone. Fingers crossed it was not one of those terminal falls. At times like this, you need to be calm and make the right decision but do it quickly. Richard thought he could scramble up the steep slabs above.

After a swift chat with Richard, we agreed that he would try to get around the fall, and I would follow Sten into… Well, I had no idea… Richard grabbed a throw line. He was 6 m up the slabs before I had my spray deck on. I heard a shriek, looking round to see Richard slipping back down, ending up beside me. Unscathed, he climbed again.

It was a risky choice to follow Sten, a MOT for me. But the thought of Sten being pinned or swimming in a deep pool, over more falls, needing help, drove me on. Deep breath, paddle, speed, boof, and land flat would give the best chance. The drop was so kind, as I descend it gives that feeling of air, into a soft and aerated flat landing, before I bobbed through the froth in the pool. I was relieved to find Sten sitting on a 25 cm wide log, jammed across the river, paddle in his hand, kayak by his feet. Richard shouted from above. All is OK, Sten explained. He went over the fall with no speed and pencilled deep into the fall, but the rope got tangled around his paddle so he could not roll.

Richard soon plopped over the drop to join us, relieved, and a big lesson learnt. More fun falls and easier water led to a large field.

At the end of the field, the unrunnable falls were to be found. If Sten had gone over the first fall here there would have been a different story.

Jori After the epic of the previous day on the Frya, we decided to go for something a bit easier where we could all paddle together. Not too far away the Jori, a tributary of the Lagen graded at 4 seemed to be the ideal choice. Indeed it proved to be. Starting at Ned Reindol (30 kroner toll), the Jori gave us 10 km of grade 3 to 4, almost continuous with the odd section that made you work a little harder. The river flows into a scenic gorge and remains challenging without being desperate. At the end of the gorge, we portaged a large weir. This had only taken us 2.5 hours.

Lora We next found ourselves by the Lora at Rusti, where it flows in places through a shallow gorge with many overhanging and undercut cliffs. Class 3 to 4, is mostly runnable on site, with egress at Haukrusti. Our 'Elverpaddling 'guidebook suggested that the falls were dangerous, so we hoped for some good photos. The guidebook said the '*next 4 km had uncertain information, though probably rather difficult.*'

The water seemed to flow at a reasonable level. The walking was rough but soon we found the falls.

This is one of those falls that you can only dream about: more slabby than vertical but big enough to get lots of adrenaline flowing, just by looking at it. At the top, around a corner, a series of small drops of grade 3+ composed the entrance rapid to a wide left-hand bend. This led straight into a channel inclined at about 30°, some 60 m long with a rooster tail in the middle. It looked intimidating. The bottom part consisted of a 6 m concave drop, vertical at the bottom, into a deep still pool. Closer inspection seemed to present no real hazards in the water but each part was difficult in itself, but strung together... did we have the skill? did we have the bottle?

We threw a few logs in to check out the rooster tail that protruded from the flow down the slabs. The logs went straight through, so there were no more excuses.

Falls of Lora – top section

Falls of Lora – bottom half

Testing the flow with logs

A stunning bright rainbow graced the tops of the spruce to end an excellent day – would it be gold tomorrow.?

The river below the falls at Haukrusti.

After a sleepless night, thinking about the falls, visualising possible routes over and over again and imagining what following the lines would entail. In ten morning I was still undecided iid I would paddle the falls. We set off for the ingress just upstream from Rusti. The river here seemed at low flow otherwise we would have gone further upstream. At Rusti, the rapids were tricky as the river cliffs consisted of layered flakes, many of which were often undercut. The following 6 km, grade 3-4 with easier sections, we paddled easily as a group but I recall noting how the usual river banter was missing. the focus was on what lay downstream. All looking out for each other, we became immersed in the river, the forest and the landscape, contemplating the falls ahead. My thoughts were absorbed in what may lie ahead. I had never previously considered doing such a large complex fall.

Falls of Lora, top slide

Too soon we arrived at Haukrusti falls. More inspections of the slabs and falls brought our attention to the awkward flow at the bottom where the water slammed into the left wall before being deflected around a corner into an eddy before the main fall at the bottom.

Decisions were made. Do it in two parts; first make the eddy, where safety lines could be in place, then rest the safety line for the bottom fall. Cameras set a MOT and off I went. The top of the falls is out of sight from the slab, so the stepped grade 3+ entry needed care and leads directly to the top of the slab, which seems to suck you in.

I round the corner, accelerate rapidly, I try to maintain balance – wow, so fast, leaning ever so slightly on the trailing paddle for some stability, the rooster tail hits me, right in the face, but just as I expect to be pinned on the back of my kayak by the force, the spray passes like a very powerful shower. The wall at the bottom accelerates towards me. I am convinced that I can't follow the water around the bend. I brace for the collision, but edge my kayak and steer away, the impact never happens. I am washed around the corner into the eddy with a ridiculous lean to counteract the speed of the breakout and avoid a capsize. Adrenaline is just yummy. Talk about being on a high, I was floating in more than one way, eager for more. Richard followed in a similar fashion.

Throw lines repositioned and still up on adrenaline.

I launch from the eddy and force a way into and across the swiftly moving water, large standing waves hide the route. I float over them. As the gradient steepens, I aim left of the middle, it gets steeper again, over a slight bulge in the waves and its free fall for what seems like ages.

The water is so aerated, it's difficult to tell when the air stops and the water begins. On down and down until I feel my kayak rotate. It seems to be stationary for a while, still, motionless, amongst all that energy, a delicate balance of gravity pulling down versus buoyancy with lifting; a surreal experience if there ever was one.

Dare I continue!

No going back

Falls of Lora, Bottom drop.

My senses are so clear and acute, I open my eyes to see clear, green water; bubbles everywhere. No noise, deadly quiet, just the feel of bubbles trickling upward across my face. It must be like this inside an aero bar. I see bubbles, where is up? As the realisation hits me that I am upside down, buoyancy begins to win its battle with gravity. My paddle instinctively moves into position for a roll, I rise to the surface, the boat steadies and I roll up, to cheers from the others elated at myself and the experience. There is nothing better than this. This is being alive.

Richard goes right

Richard followed, but not fancying the prolonged submersion he decides to paddle Stens' Dancer instead of his shorter Topolino. He headed far right. Falls down the fall at a slight angle. The nose of the Dancer hit the eddy at the base of the fall adjacent to the frothing mess, the speed of his fall powered him into the eddy, almost avoiding getting his deck wet. It was quite remarkable.

After the Haukrusti falls the river grade eases to class 3 as we float away consumed by the river. I wallow in residual adrenaline.

Driva As we moved north the weather deteriorated to drizzle. The Driva was our next target. After starting at Melem the first kilometre had many sharp rocks. Then the river entered a small gorge without presenting any real problems the paddling was fun. We paddled a 2 m ledge on the right before the difficulties eased. Several more tricky rapids kept us amused. The girls paddled everything on sight and felt they had improved their skills and confidence a lot. Having decided it was time to play pooh sticks, We all rafted up, then let go and with no paddling allowed, it was fun for a while, being at the fate of the current. Unfortunately, Richard became caught on a submerged rock, watching his dipping and rolling in the cold water provided much amusement, but brought the game to an end. Just above the bridge at Ishol, the water flows through a very confined channel, where broaching on frothy boils in the tight twists seemed to look the most likely outcome, so we portaged.

The following day saw Richard, Sten and I return to the bridge to attempt the Graura gorge of the Driva, surely one of the great gorges of Europe. On the gauge, 2.4 m seemed a good level. Drifting on the tranquil water from the bridge gave no hint of what was to come. The road is 270 m above the river for much of its length, so having set off we were committed. Soon powerful, the river led us to steep, long rapids full of jagged boulders and huge holes. We portage on the right. The confluence with the river Vindola marked the beginning of a long and continuous grade 4–5. The left side looked easier so we took it, paddling tight lines, without having the possibility of remembering a specific route. We kept close together and made frequent use of the eddies. Our easier line simply stopped at an event horizon. We attempted to inspect the next section, but getting out on the left side wasn't an option. Crossing the river looked decidedly dubious and we concluded that the description in the guidebook was correct, 'recce is difficult and portage impossible'. We managed to scramble onto a boulder to get a view of the top of at least the first part. I volunteered to be probe and hopefully with fortune favouring the brave. Staying about 20 m from the bank, I wound my way through the maze of boulders, avoiding holes and bursting stoppers as I fought my way through. Pleased to be at the bottom the easiest route was now obvious, but there was no way of communicating with the others as they couldn't see me. Soon Richard appeared. I signalled to him to go left but he hadn't seen me. He initially headed for a messy route full of choss but then made a clever route choice back across to the middle of the river. As he turned the chossy rocks he swung through 180°. His Topolino slid onto a large flat boulder, the downstream end of which unfortunately ended in an upstream bedrock incline. His slide came to an abrupt halt and water flowed over his body forcing Richard onto his back deck. Ten seconds of trying to extract himself with his paddle made no difference. I was helpless, there was nothing I could do to help him. Sten was not even aware of the situation, sitting at the top of the rapid and even if he had been aware, he couldn't have helped anyway.

Richard now tried to release his deck, but in the middle of class 5 rapid in an inescapable gorge is not a good place to swim. He had no choice as the force of the water pinned him on his back deck and he couldn't reach the release loop on his deck. He struggled, until somehow, eventually, he strained forward enough to release the deck. Immediately filling his kayak with water. The extra weight dislodged the boat, so he slid from his entrapment. Relief swept over me as I prepared to rescue him. Without his deck on, Richard paddled his 'Topolino bathtub' down the rapid to the bank without my help.

Richard had shown a shrewd awareness of the possibilities, unusual in one so young. Sten followed without incident.

The difficulties soon eased to a swift but very classy grade 4+. The boulders were more rounded and the channels more defined. Still with many holes and boulders to avoid, but some classic paddling. We made swift progress. Lunch was taken on a boulder that spanned the width of the river and provided our last portage adjacent to a narrow 5 m slide into a deep recirculating hole. It was with some relief to see the road descending towards the river, The river lost some of its power as the gradient of the river bed eased. With the end in sight, we could relax, pleased to have survived, our skills tested and utilised to the full.

Grovu

The road to our final river, the Grovu, our guidebook informed us '*the road ends at a farm near Jenstad with some impressive waterfalls, 100 m or so each, stick out in this wonderful valley*'.

Portaging 10 minutes down to the river warms you up. The river is continuous grade 4 - 5 full of boulders and without relent for 3 km. Many routes are viable, all read and run. Resting is possible, with skill, in the many small eddies.

After two weeks of paddling, we felt strong and confident, skills honed, and river reading skills tuned. We cruised this river without problems, following it back to our rented hytte on the river bank.

Even Norwegian sheep are a little different

Is this where the Troll lives? Falls near Jenstad

We broke the long drive back to the UK with a spot of canogining. Steep snowfields at the top of one of the passes lead to a small lake. We constructed a ramp to increase the thrills before being forced to quit, after a few icy dunkings in the small glacial lake.

I made a successful attempt on our Scooby snack record, with 15 different fillings in one sandwich, everything from cheese to sardines, jam to marmite, lettuce, baked beans and tomato puree.

We drove past potential adventures, some beautiful rivers, one where a waterfall slides 30 m down slabs from one lake into another.

I had applied my skills and pushed my limits. I was content with the way I dealt with the challenges I encountered.

Exploring in the Jungle

Costa Rica (July 1990)

Sten Sture, Angela Sture, Pip Line, Chris Walker, Jim Stilling, Graham Burns, Graham Jones

After the trip down the Grand Canyon, I found myself sitting in the Flagstaff, Arizona library, browsing old copies of the American Paddler magazine. There were lots of articles, but two caught my eye and both were about paddling in Costa Rica. During the next few months of research, I located a guidebook and two contacts. One Rafael Gallo in San Jose, whose company, Rio Tropicales, would hire us kayaks and provide raft support on a 4-day Rio General trip. The other was Ken, an American who had a guest house in Sarapiqui. With information from the 'Rivers of Costa Rica' guidebook by Rafael and the articles from the American River Runner magazine. The trip seemed would be feasible, as most rivers could be run as one day trip. After an abortive attempt to go to Costa Rica in 1989, I found a bit more enthusiasm and drive to bring together a team of 8, to make what we believe, was the first British kayaking trip to Costa Rica.

Chris, Pip and I went out before the others and had a varied but excellent time walking around the jungle, camping on beaches, climbing volcanoes, testing out the local delicacies and spotting wildlife. The others arrived a week later, so we stayed in a hotel near the airport. The following day we hired a van and drove to the viewpoint of Rincon de la Vieja, an extinct volcano. We were dressed for the 30°C heat of San Jose, so we were caught out by the near-freezing conditions near the summit. That evening our meal was accompanied by 90p cocktails and a wobbling lamppost, not caused by too many cocktails, but by a minor Earth tremor. The following day, during a very soggy walk along a jungle trail we saw no wildlife at all. That afternoon, we visited the reptile house to swot up on poisonous snakes, that we might encounter later on. Finally, we visited Rio

Tropicales, to sort out our kayaks. We had a choice of Dancer, Canyon or Aeroquatic, so we were pleased.

The following morning Raphael sorted the food and logistics for the 4-day trip, before picking us up from our hotel. We drove for five hours over the mountains to the valley of the Rio General. The bus left us with Rafael our guide, and author of the guidebook, Tori with his raft and Pete the local hanger-on/helper, with enough food for the trip.

We planned to pick Rafael's local knowledge about the rivers we intend to paddle on the rest of our trip.

Rio General. Setting off about 2:00 p.m., we soon found ourselves playing on some big, bouncy, class 3 waves. There were a few of those pour-over stoppers that you avoid if you can. Unfortunately, Angela didn't, but she did enjoy swimming in the warm water. We made camp each day at about 4:00 p.m., before the afternoon deluge, just in time to erect the tarp shelter, which funnelled the rain allowing us to shower in the cooler water.

The evening meals were accompanied by cocktails and several hours of lightning.

A local crosses the Rio General

The next two days along the Rio General were long, with many rapids. Chirripo Grande stands out. A hard ferry glide was needed to miss big boulders and avoid pushy holes to gain the best line through bouncy waves. 'Michael's 3 Miles' turned out to be only a few hundred metres of play waves and stoppers. 'Screaming Right-Hand Turn' had big breaking waves with a playable pillow right in the middle of the flow.

Another fabulous play wave the BREW (**b**est **r**ear-**e**nd **w**ave) was at a perfect level. The breaking top made it so very playable, providing slow but predictable bow or tail dips. We spent the best part of two hours exploring its possibilities.

*Author surfing on the BREW **b**est rear-end wave*

We saw many iguanas basking on the rocks on the bank and in the main flow. One named rapid 'Go Left and Die' or was it 'Go Left or Die'. It would have been useful to remember the name accurately. It turned out not as bad as it sounded, however, the left involved a drop of 2 m into a nasty mess; whilst the right was a big, bouncy, fast wave train, so we headed right.

Next came the pièce de résistance. At a tight right bend in the river, an angled rocky reef on the left constricted the flow. Behind the reef, there is a still eddy. As the water accelerates past the end of the reef the difference in flow rates creates a mobile whirlpool that spins as it migrates downstream. A rare feature on rivers. You could surf a gentle wave to the left, before nudging onto the stopper, before your boat spins around in the ever-variable wash cycle. With correct timing, the spin becomes vertical, sometimes facing down, occasionally facing up. The whirlyness sucks you down, spinning, kayak and all, sometimes below water level. You spin downstream in the vortex before the energy is dissipated, thus releasing you. So good, so very good you have to go round for more, many times.

A rear spin-down during the wash cycle on the Rio General whirlpool

He he

Such fun, floating around, paddling in, popping out, again and again. Exactly as the guidebook says *'giggling the afternoon away'*, after two hours and we still didn't want to leave.

The evening's entertainment became annoying Mimosa trees, whose leaves retract when touched. The rafting team climbed trees to collect orchids, which they took back to base with them.

Morning brought us some easy rapids and finally to 'Chachalaca', a fine, scary wave if you're brave enough. One of those standing huge waves with an unpredictable crashing top.

Winning or losing in Chachalaca?

Maintaining control is very difficult, wiping out is easy, and enders (summersaults), maybe more than one, are not uncommon.

Chachalaca played with you, not the other way around. Sten popped his spray deck whilst in the wave and Jim managed to get sucked out of his boat, disappearing downstream for 30 m, located only by him sticking his paddle vertically into the air. We paddled with several otters alongside us later that day, before the difficulties eased.

After a long, hot wait, sitting in the river, we were taken back to San Jose where we picked up two Isuzu four-wheel-drive trucks. Space for four people in the front cab and room for all of our gear and kayaks in the back. We drive north to a small town called La Virgen, Rancho Leona our destination; run by an American called Ken, who had moved to Costa Rica and lived there for many years. He was also a paddler and allowed to stay at his house for a fee. He gave us some good tips on the rivers.

Sarapiqui

Sarapiqui. 22 km grade 5-4 then 3. The Sarapiqui flowed past Ken's ranch, so it became our first choice. It was our first trip alone in the jungle. Virgin jungle is adjacent to the river, and not much opportunity to inspect if you need. There are no houses, and no roads until the next bridge. The first 12 km at a steep 25 m/km was fast and very challenging. The river flowed through the beautiful undisturbed jungle, and wildlife abounds. To experience the jungle habitat in its raw state was so enchanting, and engaging. The first rapid lasted 8 km before a proper eddy was found. Many more long rapids followed with 90° turns, many ending with cushions flowing onto cliff faces.

Pena Blancas, A two-hour trip from Poco Sol found us temporarily lost, until, after much guesswork, we eventually located a put it near La Virgen. Four of us set off the following day down the Pena Blancas, the 'White Willie' river as we called it. Again continuous white water kept coming and coming. Fifteen kilometres grade 4 or 3 from start to finish. Kilometres of boulder garden led to wider stretches, again through virgin jungle, with sulphurous pools on the river banks. About halfway we stopped to allow the rest of the group to join us. We were rewarded by seeing some bright, orange, poison arrow frogs. From the bridge, at San Isicho the water was constant grade 3 until the river divided again and again and again until the channels were only a metre wide. Take your pick and go for it. Just like a blind maze. We almost missed the takeout in a field! oops. The next stop was the Caribbean 80 kilometres away. While we awaited the shuttle, a local gaucho guy approached us on his horse. Angela fancied a go, having had some experience many years before. The horse looked quite frisky, but she soon had it tamed and trotted around the field. Chris decided he was next. The horse just sat still. He couldn't make it go, '*squeeze its ribs with your legs*' came the advice, nothing, '*Try squeezing harder,*' the horse bolted. Galloping away in a straight line, only to turn a right angle just next to a bamboo stand. The horse veered right, but Chris went straight on to disappear in the bamboo. We almost fell over with laughter. It was a few minutes before Chris emerged. He walked back slowly, leading the horse to its owner; the rest of us still laughing.

Toro 17 km of 4+. Ken, our friendly American said he would come with us on the Toro, so he drove us to the put-in, four miles upstream of the one suggested in the book. We then discovered this top section had only been paddled once before. Some of our team had a MOT and decided to get on lower down. It was a serious proposition: some difficult grade 4 water with vertical conglomerate gorge walls, inescapable, care was needed. This was no place for an incident. Despite this we managed to paddle rapids on sight, leapfrogging as the probe. The surprises came thick and fast, so probing was edgy, to say the least. On one steep grade 4+, a couple of Scrimblies caused two of the team to roll. On reaching the put-in suggested in the book, two others joined us by sliding down the waste from a pig farm. The rapids were mostly boulder ledges, which steepened as you went down. Each one ended with a drop over larger boulders. Pinning was a constant worry, made more sinister by vultures gazing from the bank, awaiting their next meal. Graham took a nasty swim, bruising his back after colliding with a round boulder After a subsequent swim, we saw him lying atop his upturned kayak to avoid a repeat, very clever. Occasionally, we were accompanied by iguanas swimming down beside us. The rapids are continuous, and with little time to rest, we found lots of super, but scary stuff.

Toro Amarillo. We promised ourselves an easier day so we only paddled 6 km of 3 with 4+ on the Toro Amarillo. The highlights were a sloth and paddling during a thunderstorm. We then took a long drive, before finding ourselves, at the only 'hotel' in Guapilles. You might say, you wouldn't stop there by choice. The locals were cagey, watching our every move. A very warm night was spent avoiding cockroaches, or large spiders and bedbugs, depending upon which room you were lucky enough, not to be able to sleep in.

Sucio. The following day, it was on to the rusty-coloured Sucio (dirty river) 9 km 3-4+ 30 m per km. A yellow ochre colouring of iron salts washed down from the volcanic slopes in the river's headwaters, tainted the water. The river rocks and boulders were coated with a very rough surface and the salts had killed all the vegetation on the river bank. The water volume was quite large and the riverbed was steep, so the rapids were pushy. As the kilometres passed the difficulties seemed to increase, and the stoppers were more grabby. Chris took a swim and was glad of his chin guard on his helmet. A nice clear tributary doubled the volume so the rapids became wilder but deeper. Only one inspection was needed after that. Another great adventure.

We spent two days on the Caribbean coast where we rented a smart chalet, just north of Leman. Sunbathing on the beach, eating fresh fruit, and being shaded by palm trees is bliss. It was too hot to stay in the open for long, but add 2m surf rolling in a warm sea and you maybe have paradise.

Pacuare. Our next move was to a mountaintop hotel, Pochotel which gave excellent views over the Reventazon valley. From here a two-hour drive to the put-in on the Pacuare. Twenty-five kilometres grade 3 with 4(5). The river flowed across the middle of nowhere. Finding the put-in was difficult as it involved a half-mile of carrying kayaks down small tracks to the river through the jungle.

Once on the river, it became obvious the level was high. Care was needed as it was meaty stuff, with holes to avoid. Angela was grabbed by one, which then added Chris as he tried to rescue her. Many rapids, followed by beautiful waterfalls and impressive wildlife, with vines hanging everywhere. After a few hours, we stopped for lunch but were unable to work out how far we had gone. We knew that Upper Hucas rapid and falls at 16 km were yet to come. Soon after lunch, the rapids became pushier, requiring precise manoeuvring, with many huge holes to avoid. As the river narrowed and the percentage of boiling water increased.

Hucas falls Rio Pacuare

Soon we were up at Upper Hucas, only 80 m long but with random holes, boils and boulders. Tricky, OTI, we all made it through despite going different ways. The rapids of Lower Hucas were a different proposition, with only one feasible route which involved punching at least three big holes formed on slides between boulders. Some portaged but those that tried made it successfully, it was more intimidating than difficult. More big wave rapids followed, which helped the kilometres pass quickly. The river eased until we approached Dos Mantras, a narrow defile 200 m long guarded by grade 4 rapids. The vertical sides of the river are stripped of vegetation by debris falling from the blasting for a new dam. This was so disappointing as it meant work had started on damming the river, which would flood most of its excellent rapids. Another long tiring day was more taxing due to the remoteness of the journey.

Reventazon. The next day we paddled a 20 km section of Reventazon, a big volume grade 3, which was mud brown in colour, making it impossible to see the rocks. Disaster almost struck as we approached a dead tree, across the river by an island. A difficult manoeuvre to try to pass by its fallen branches at this water level, with no stopping before it.

The evening was seen out with 3 bottles of Bacardi Gold. The morning saw us with thick heads. Our next plan was to do the 14 km class 5 section of the Reventazon. The river gauge indicates 240 well above the maximum level we had been recommended. Having viewed the biggest rapids our hesitation was justified by lines of huge river-wide holes. We inspected the rest of the river from a 90 minute train ride which cost 2p each. We decided to pass. It was too much for us.

Grande di Orosi. The last day of paddling was a blast, on the Grande di Orosi. A 6 km class 4 run, with continuous white water. Again a bit pushy, but superb lines, a fine last run in Costa Rica.

It was a risk to visit a country relatively unknown for paddling. The unusual surroundings enhanced the rewards, so making the effort more than worthwhile. Using local knowledge proved a good strategy to get our trip off to a great start. Being bold in our choices played its part in delivering a most enjoyable fun trip for all.

Author beautifying in Costa Rican hot spring mud

The Bio Bio Calls

Chile (December 1990)

Robin Everingham, Andy Hall, Marcus Bailie, Phil Bibby + Lisa (an American lady)

What next? The Christmas break from work, allowed 3 weeks to fit in a trip. The Bio Bio rose to the top of my list. At the time considered one of the top ten kayaking challenges in the world. I had a lucky break when I found an advertisement from Eric Leaper, an American who had done some exploring in Chile, offering a trip. This opened up possibilities. Robin Everingham and I were keen, and soon Andy Hall, Marcus Bailie and Phil Bibby had decided to join us. Two long flights saw us in Santiago loading the kit into Eric's van before driving south.

We visited a class 3, **Rio Maipo,** for a long warm-up paddle, before heading further south to the **Rio Claro**, which hid the beautiful Siete Tasas – 7 teacups, in the bottom of a deep basalt gorge. Once you are in, you are in, You have to finish, a short run of seven blind falls, each ending in an ever so deep, clear, pool, each one a dream. All together a classic section.

The last fall of 10 m is a near vertical drop, hard to boof due to the angle of the lip. It certainly felt like 10 m as you descended into the deep pool of water, enough time to get that roller coaster stomach feeling. The impact slapped my face, forcing water up inside my nostrils. More scary than the falls was the egress.

We paddled down a relatively easy canyon for a short distance, before making a micro eddy and egressing up the near vertical basalt cliffs to safety. If you miss the eddy a series of hard falls led to a final unpaddled 27 m drop - one to be missed.

The first fall of the teacup section, Rio Claro

The following day found us setting up camp in a field by the **Bio Bio** river. At the time, reputedly one of the classic big water runs in the world.

Flowing about 15000 cfs this December, it was going to be predictably scary. Three sections were of interest. The first is an upper basalt gorge. Second, came the 1000 waterfalls section, so called due to the number of streams tumbling down the basalt walls. Third, the Royal Flush section. Our first run through the upper section started easily enough, but soon we were faced with a 1 km section of continuous large grade 3/4 water. Scouting from the bank confirmed our original thoughts, no chicken run here, all routes possible. We decided to stay close to the right bank in case of a mishap. We ran it as a team, well strictly speaking, as seven individuals pretending to be a team. Phew, no mishaps, confidence was rising in proportion to the smiles.

The river eased for a while, and then an obvious mid-stream van-sized boulder split the flow. Either side seems feasible. Somehow, Lisa managed to get a little behind. We had all bobbed by when somehow Lisa headed straight for the boulder '*Where is she going?*' up over the guarding cushion, then fell over and down the downstream side. A MOT for Lisa, she became engulfed in the confusion stopper and boils. After what seemed like ages, but was probably only a few seconds, she passed through still upright. She was understandably a little shaken, Glad it wasn't me, but then it wouldn't be. This was an unnecessary mistake, a wake-up call to be alert at all times for us all.

Soon we were at Lost Yak rapid, a class 5 mega beast. So-called after one of the first descenders lost his kayak in this rapid. I dislike it when rapids are named, the chosen names rarely inspire confidence. The middle line in Lost Yak flows through far too many big boulders to remember a specific route; all routes flow through or close to massive holes. The chicken run, far left for us, was still pushy, still with holes to avoid, but at least you could plan a line and locate it whilst paddling. Not far downstream Lava South (Lava North is the hardest rapid on the Colorado Grand Canyon) was another grade 5 super-mess. This time the right side took 20% of the flow, a class 4 possibility. The left side saw 80% of the flow accumulate over a ledge into a 6 m high stopper wall, to go this way looked like certain death.

Fortunately, a pointed rock was relatively easy to spot, something to aim for, just where you needed to be to the right.

We ran it in groups of 3, to allow others to take photos. Robin, myself and Eric found a cool route, going right, avoiding the main event. Phil went next but decided he was going solo. Unbelievably we watched, as he went left of the pointed boulder.

No way. From our vantage on the shore, we could see there was no way to make it back right. My level of concern grew! The river Scrimblies decided to play.

Just down from the pointy rock, a stopper. It looked small compared to the maelstrom downstream. But still, it did what stoppers do; it stopped Phil; threw him around a bit, two front loops, oh my god!

He rolled and is flushed out, into the next equally large hole. No way! No way! Phil side-surfed for a minute or so but eventually made his way to the right and escaped, directly into the main flow of that huge river-wide monster.

The start of Phil's trouble, he should be right of that boulder.

Shared words of '*that's it, he's dead*' wafted above the roar of the flow. At the mercy of the river, Phil was now no more than a cork. At the mercy of the flow, he was pushed down into that hole, where you just never ever want to go.

He disappeared... what! How can that be? He was flushed through, upright, up the wall of white, twice the length of his 4m kayak. For what seemed like a long time but maybe only a minute, he was thrown about but stayed upright. He's going backwards... to die... no he's stopped. Somehow the exploding frothiness of unpredictability was holding him on the stopper face, just above the main recirculation.

Forced onto the boils from the cliff

Phil was now paddling forward like a madman possessed, up the face of the exploding frothiness – going nowhere.

The river will win, but he gets pushed towards the left bank, where the hole is steepest. The far end is closed out by massive cushion boils formed on the cliff side…there is only one end here. Out of luck, Phil is out of range of help, all we can do is watch. Unbelievably, a massive surge from the stopper wall throws Phil up onto the boil below the cliff.

Now there is edging and there is edging. Almost on his side, Phil's paddling instinct kicked in. Somehow his head remained where he can breathe. We noticed the boil was somehow preventing him from moving downstream. But slowly it relented and allowed him to go just past the hole.

Almost through

Another reprieve, more exploding waves force him back onto the boil. This time just support strokes were not enough, downstream effort was needed. Only 3m gained but it is enough. Still excessively turbulent, the massive hole is passed but a long wall of huge breaking cushion plays with his kayak nudging it to a 'calmer' grade 4. A frantic ferry glide, and he's made it. Astonished, we ran to congratulate Phil on his fortune and skill. Seemingly unperturbed, inside he was shaking, philosophically mellow. *'Didn't see that spike rock'* he retorted. That was a big MOT for Phil, that should and would have ended differently.

The Bio runs through a series of basalt gorges, with 100 m walls numerous waterfalls and views to the snow-capped, 3050 m volcano Callaqui; It is simply a stunning vista that just keeps rolling. Every corner brings a new view.

The 1000 waterfalls canyon

We found some hot springs at the end of the day's run, just next to our campsite. Reflecting on the events of the day, we felt humbled and fortunate to still be a full team. Individually, we had gained in confidence, and as a group, we fed off each other's enthusiasm. Tomorrow was the Royal Flush.

The Royal Flush canyon begins with some big bouncy class 3 before the river narrowed, an outcrop on the right, and a bouldery beach on the left, inspect. Seems OK, it's big. Yes big. But a big breaking wave, with a long green tongue as the lead-in. The Green Wall is its name. Someone shared a thought, '*it's going to be like getting eaten*'

Setting off, in pairs, adrenaline pumping, I have no MOT as I am positive about the outcome, *I check my knee bracing is tight, ferry out 30 m and turn right. Here I go, down the tongue, hit the wave head-on, lean forward, and place my paddle on the front deck. The massive 3 m wave peaks high over me. Everything goes green, then I fly out of the downstream side, over six big standing waves, and it's done.* I am amazed to still be upright. Five of our team of seven rolled.

The author is about to be consumed by the green wall

The 1000 waterfall canyon soon follows, only class 3, it is a time to relax and contemplate, as it then leads to the Royal Flush canyon.

The sequence starts with Ace, a long but straightforward bouncy 3+ wave train. Around the corner, Suicide King, we inspect. A sizeable drop, 5 m in one rapid, Down the middle, over the boil line onto a huge, but smooth boil, where water wells up from the vertical left bank bedrock.

The King, entry

From on the water, looking downstream, it looks serious, but from the bank, there is an obvious route. Over the edge of the boil, turn right, then down a long steep green tongue and under an exploding, but straightforward wave. The crux is finding the weakness in the boil line into the smoothness beyond. All goes well without mishap. It proves to be much easier than expected.

King exit

The Queen of Hearts is next. Tricky, with a large folding wave, but more mellow than the King, we read and ran it without incident.

Queen of Hearts

Last but not least, as the saying goes. The local Mapuche call it Salto, or Legendary Falls. Its legendary status seemed justified. One-eyed Jack, one-eyed for a reason. The river collides with a massive boulder, then steepens as it crashes over 3 ledges, each with a river-wide hole that will stop you.

Each has a maybe line, where occasionally, a tongue might just allow the breaking foam walls to be breached. One would be a challenge, two seems too much, but three, surely not? Each stopper was bigger than the previous one.

Occasionally, there is a short-lived break in the white walls, as a minor tongue develops weaknesses, but these are far from being lined up. Timing of the key move is crucial since the water is too variable and too unpredictable to rely on as a marker. The only identified point is your relative position to a 5 m cliff on the right bank. Well, I guess we are here, so… If I hadn't been scared to death, it would have been fun; MOT to be sure.

Time to plan a way through, I consider following the flow! *Can I find a line? Yes! Will I make it? Maybe!* Can I follow that plan on the water? Who knows! Robin and I look at each other and nod. I wonder why my mouth was dry! Must be the heat. Ferry out, the kayak turned left. What am I doing? Too late now. Why am I doing this?

My tactic is to lead left, accelerate towards the first stopper fast and straight, lean forward, reach far into the wave and pull hard and through! Momentary relief; now moving quickly 10m right, until I am 8m from the cliff wall, where hopefully the timing of the occasional weakness will coincide with my arrival at the second river-wide muncher. The current pulls me faster into the second stopper, I lean forward, and water envelops my kayak, but I keep paddling, my timing is perfect, two down one to go. But then doom beckons.

I quickly try to move right a few metres. I need to get there early, so I can line up for the final nastiness, but waves rise and fall to impede my move. The flow feels so fast. Stay calm; deep breath; better; I turn my kayak so it faces directly downstream. As I plunge into the third hole my forward motion slows, as the water crashes onto my head, I sink into the wave, which engulfs me.

I feel my stern pull down, expecting that ever so horrible, disorientating back loop; but it doesn't come. I burst from the back of the wave like a cork and negotiate the final 80m of frothiness. YES, my brain screams, I made it. Buzzing – this is why we do it! The others have more problems 2 swims, 3 rolls. Soon all the kayaks paddles and owners are reunited. We float downstream in differing states of elation.

Robin's entry of One-Eyed Jack

Eric in one-eyed Jack – first wave of 3

Paddling on downstream for another 15km, of comparatively easy water, we careered and careened through many rapids. With every passing kilometre, the river gave us a combination of its best features.

Fifty-metre-tall araucaria pine (monkey puzzle trees) are interspersed with cedar and lines of poplars. Layers of pumice and hard andesite intermittently break through the basalt walls. The flow slows, and finally, the cliffs are behind us. A volcano, whose name we are unaware of dominates the scene. There is a sense of leaving behind the wild adventure and of gliding away from the previously unknown.

The end of the Royal Flush Gorge

Armed with the knowledge of previous days, we repeat the two sections with a more relaxed atmosphere in the group. Knowing what to expect and the lines we needed to run, gave us more time to appreciate the situation. At Lost Yak, I decided a line down the middle would go. Plenty of markers to recognise, but far too many to remember for the whole 300 m. It will be read and run most of the way. Strategy is the key: I have to hit a big cushion wave on the right, in the centre of the river before a smooth tongue falls between two big holes, the right one guarded by a cushion on a 3 m boulder. The approach detail too much to recall. *It is a moving maze of unpredictability. Left and right, are a mix of breaking waves and standing waves with small holes to burst through and tongues to find. Always, I focus on that boulder, 200 m downstream. Now 100 m, soon 40 m, I see the cushion, so I know I must go left. No! I am forced right, towards the cushion. Instinct kicks in, stay calm, instant plan, brace on the cushion, I edge the kayak almost vertically. Come on you've done this so many times in surf, I tell myself.*

The cushion is bigger, more powerful than I had expected having looked from the bank, I wonder why? I hit it, at an angle. Lean onto it, and paddle inside the up-thrusting water. That is a fab brace; I feel good, but no!

Despite my speed, my edge and my brace, the force simply throws me back over to the left, capsized. Instinct kicks in, and I roll, a fast, first-time roll. I surface on the tongue between those two murky holes. Giggling, high on adrenaline, I never felt so good, that line of misadventure, so good to be close to, so pleased not to have crossed it.

The next two days passed without great incidents. We left the valley full of joy, wondering what lay further upstream. But that would have to wait for another trip. We headed for Pucon, enabling us in the next two days to descend the **Pucon** river (now called **Trancura**) and another river nearby that Eric had been spying out. For Christmas day lunch we enjoyed enchiladas, eaten in an abandoned stable full of hay.

We climbed volcano Villarica 2680m after hiring homemade crampons, made by bending and welding 6-inch nails.

Volcan Villarica

On to the **Fuy,** a fun, fast-flowing, medium-volume river. We ran the upper section, to the enticing, beautiful falls, 3 large drops. Each fall is over 10m high with too much recirculating aerated water and FWD in the pools, surely gorge monsters lurk here. We passed on the opportunity. The following day found us in a lower section just tootling along and having fun. Playing in waves, and doing some moves.

I dropped into an innocuous hole sideways for a play, it was about a boat length long. I hadn't appreciated that it was a pour-over, thus giving rather a deeper trough than expected. I sat side surfing for a few seconds, before trying an exit. *Edge on the downstream wave paddle forwards on the downstream side expecting to exit easily, but no! Try again; attempt 2. The same outcome, I bounced around in the hole. 3rd time lucky? I gain forward momentum, bow draw, pull, slice the paddle, pull again, and try to face downstream, but it's not letting go.*

My 4th attempt is similar. Attempt 5 think! Water flows out deep, under the wave, as I capsize through the stopper, slide my hands along the paddle loom, and extend my lower blade deeper into the outflow below the hole. I feel that pull, but it's not enough, I roll up on the wave. On attempt 6 I edge my kayak less, so the kayak slides up to the top of the breaking wave, and an offside lean with a stern rudder. Yes, I spin the boat, its nose directly upstream, and my bow dives into the wave. I get vertical, the pop-up is weak and I am back, side surfing again. Attempt 7 try again, a better pop out, but still not enough to clear the holding trough. This is quite a sticky hole.

The guys on the bank have their throw lines ready. There is only one way out of here. I pull the deck and slide out of my kayak, sink into the waves, grab a throw line and get pulled to the side. The kayak surfed on its own a little longer before deciding to join me. A salutary lesson. Never relax.

Fuy Fun

148

Bedrock Heaven

Corsica (April 1992)

Chris Walker, Graham Burns

Despite all the opportunities that come with paddling big-volume water, I find it ultimately scary. I found my preference was for lower volume, steeper creeks. The Upper Tarn and Dourbie in the Central Massif of France seem so much more fun, so much more of a challenge for me. Corsica called. A long drive and a ferry took 3 days.

Corsican rivers run on the snow melt around Easter time. It is a bit of a lottery hitting the right river flows. We got lucky. Almost all the rivers are granite bedrock rivers characterised by slides, drops, boulder gardens, and narrow chutes, often in remote gorges. It's a smorgasbord of white-water possibilities. The main consideration is how remote do you want to go, and how hard do you want to be tested. The guidebooks were in German, so whatever we chose to paddle it was a bit of a lottery since we could not glean the full meaning of each description. The mountain roads are very tortuous, full of S bends and tight curves. If you drive at an average of 30 mph on them you are doing well.

Most Corsican rivers are a little like the river Etive in Scotland but on steroids. They are bedrock granite, rounded boulders, and have a steep gradient. They are very much similar in nature to the Upper Tarn and Dourbie gorges.

Day 1: We chose the **Asco** 9 km of 3-4 to begin with, then a long 500 m portage followed by a seal launch into a narrow ravine, which was like a bobsleigh run, eventually popping out through an arch. It was an alien start compared to what we were used to.

Author, on the Asco

Day 2: The **Upper Golo** 8 km of 5 with one grade 6 took us 5 hours to complete.

In the 8 km, two falls were far too tricky for us, so portages were opted for.

The author takes a tight drop on Upper Golo

Day 3: We were attracted to pictures of steep slides of the **Travo** 6 km 4-5. A boulder-filled river, continuous in its pool-drop nature. The river starts with typical Corsican bedrock and mazes of rounded boulders.

It seemed like a big reward when we arrived at the slides, 3 of them stacked one after the other; set in a unique amphitheatre of granite bedrock. Drops of 3m, 5m and 2m follow in quick succession. Each with its own still teacup pool. If you could be inspired, this was surely a place to be so.

After a kilometre or so a skull and crossbones plaque indicated a portage. Truth be known, it looks much like many of the other steep bouldery sections we had already run. However, the sign indicated that a paddler had died, pinned some years before in a boulder sieve on the 3m drop just below. This seemed to put everyone off, so we portaged along a ledge. This ended with us throwing the boats 3m into a deep clear pool, jumping after them, and swimming 10m across the pool to a shingle corner. Downstream we portaged twice more where gneiss rock barriers blocked the flow.

Author on Travo top slide in the amphitheatre

152

Day 4: **Taravo** 9 km 4-5 The start is in a bedrock canyon, with a mellow grade 2, then more bedrock falls and pools.

Taravo fun

Day 5: **Liamone** - lower.10 km 4-5, We found many steep bouldery falls all paddleable and a 4 m slab requiring a sharp right move as you drop into a narrower section at the bottom.

1 km before the end a klamm, a vertical-sided slot canyon, held siphons. The 250 m portage is rewarded by a fine seal launch to finish off the klamm.

Day 6: **Upper Liamone** 8 km grade 5 then 4.,

Liamone

Day 7: **Vecchio** 8 km grade 4–5. We found ourselves on the Vecchio. The DKV guidebook likens it to the Upper Tarn gorge. Full of bedrock slides and steep boulder gardens seems to be a fitting last challenge.

Vecchio

Some years later, I visited Corsica again with Richard Evans, Steve Rogers, Alistar Paley and Paul McClintock but found low water, so we opted to repeat the Lower Liamone, Vecchio and Taravo. Our last day found us on the Rizzanese 14 km–6 km grade 5 then 8 km grade 3. A little scrapey it would be fair to say, but the lure was great. Lots of typical bedrock drops and bouldery falls. Soon after there was a tricky narrow slot followed by a 6 m river-wide ledge, which we portaged. Shortly, another 6 m fall led to the main event. The 10 m vertical drop. No portage, so it is either paddle it or throw your boat in and jump after. The pool is well deep, so we all opted to paddle. I tend to put my paddle along the length of the kayak when doing falls of this height. It reduces the resistance when hitting the water at the bottom. Although the water at the base of the falls is aerated, landing flat from 10 m is not to be recommended. I was volunteered to go first, getting my sinuses thoroughly washed. Then came Richard and Steve, with no problems. Alistar landed flat and completely disappeared. First, the bow of his boat surfaced, then the stern! Where was Alastair? His head appeared. Something didn't look right. Howls of laughter ensued as we realised his kayak had snapped underneath his seat. At right angles to its length. He was sat in a V-shaped boat, each end level with his head, interesting! We helped Alastair onto a nearby ledge and waited for Paul, who emerged from the bubbles with a broken paddle. More chortling to be heard. Then realisation kicked in, we were deep in the Rizzanese gorge, and the way out was downstream. We had forgotten the spare split paddles. One thing was in our favour, Alistar was able to loan Paul his paddles. One problem is sorted.

We had to leave the split boat on a ledge not far from the falls. Alistar descended the rest of the run through a mad combination of swimming some rapids, running along the bank, climbing along cliffs and even sitting on the back of a raft of 2 kayaks being towed by the 2 others.

Our main concern was that eventually, the split kayak would be flushed out of the gorge and be found, sparking off a rescue situation. So, after sorting the shuttle, the priority was to inform the local police. They didn't seem bothered. It seems like a lost kayak was a 'usual scenario in Corsica'

Two days later on the Upper Liamone, Paul was probe, when he decided to get out and inspect. He saw a slab slide which required a right-angle turn at its end whilst dropping into a narrow slot.

Paul gave the thumbs up. The slab was fun, but the slot was so aerated I sank up to our armpits. It was so narrow I could not use my paddles effectively. A moment of angst ensued before the slot released me. The others follow down by one, each sampling this undesirable experience. Having seen everyone else have the same problem, Paul decided to potage down the slab and avoid the issue. That evening, back at the tents, Paul was found guilty of culpable sandbagging.

Somewhere Steep and Narrow

The Lech Gorges (August 1992)

Richard Evans, Nick Mortimer, Steve Rogers, Dave Hansen, Steve Lawrence

The Lech gorges are a committing prospect. Once you are in, you are in until you reach the end! The only prospect of escape is after 8 km, between the two gorges which require an 800 m climb up steep wooded slopes. As the river descends the road rises away to the north, engendering a real sense of isolation, commitment and adventure. Added to this the second of the gorges is often vertical-sided for long stretches, and many of the falls must be run on-site amongst the many boulder gardens. Add to this log jams and avalanche plugs and you have the lot. Oh, except if you go too early in the season the glacier plugs have not melted enough and the river sumps underneath them. Even if they are melted, the glacial caves beneath them always look ready to collapse.

To begin, it is all quite straightforward

The gorge narrows

As I enter the first gorge, the walls soon close in, and vertical cliffs rise high on both sides. All the way the river fills the bottom of the gorge, lapping the walls, there are no beaches.

Vertical cliffs are the bank

At times the flow is swift, but steady, with small drops and occasionally intricate lines between small boulders have to be made.

I soon develop a sense of solitude, I am going somewhere that not so many have been before, and I wonder, maybe worry, about what lies around the next corner. There is PFE for 6 more kilometres.

We have to portage a boulder choke, and we climb up and carry our kayaks around. But how do we get back in? The only way back in is an 8m seal launch.

Seal launch.

Not far into the gorge we see the top of an ice plug. Fortunately, as we float closer a gap appears underneath the plug.

The first of the avalanche plugs shows an ice cave which is the only way on.

The second plug soon follows with no chance of carrying around. It is longer than the first and dark underneath. Our anxiety grows. There is no way of telling if there is a way through. Until just upstream from the entrance, we see light and relax.

The second ice plug

Emerging from the second ice plug

An event horizon. What comes next?

Fortunately, again there is a clear way through. So we emerge from the second glacier plug feeling cut off from the rest of the world, but hey it is sunny, the river is wall to wall and we are doing fine.

Admiring the strata in the rock, I wondered why it was vertical and not horizontal. Snapping back to reality, I realised that although the cliff is not so high I wouldn't be climbing out, even if I had to!

The walls close in and flat pools lead to rapids and falls that you couldn't quite see properly until you got just above them. So many event horizons. Then, of course, there were the log jams. We were lucky as only a few trees were to be found in the gorge this year and only one of them needed to be portaged.

Tree trunks almost block the way

The tree trunks were very large as shown in this image. They have washed down the gorge with the spring melt! In some years, they form huge dams, but not this year.

In one section there was a 1m drop into a very small pool, just big enough to stop in, turn around and then accelerate past a telegraph pole-like tree wedged in the river. There was enough room to pass, but it is awkward enough, to distract you as you take the 2 m drop beside it. What a weird but wonderful place to paddle.

Occasionally, there were calmer stretches where you could rest and collect your thoughts or wonder why you were here.

A typical boulder choke

There are the boulder chokes, very tight, very naughty as you can't tell if there is a tree hidden under the water. You need to concentrate all the time. A few require portages.

Portage

At the crux of this gorge, from sitting in your kayak upstream, one simply cannot see where the water is going. There is no possibility of inspection or portage. So we stop and wait in the eddy looking at each other, wondering who is going first and which way to go.

No inspection was possible! Really! Paddling blind never brings with it a good feeling, but occasionally it is the only option.

But there is no choice: stay there forever or go with the flow. Certainly an MOT with PFE. So left over the first drop, right at the second, then down the middle, angling right to take the blind drop closest to the large angular rock on the bank. Aim right here, to avoid the suck to the left, where the flow pushes you into a recirculating eddy, which just happens to flow under a low undercut, but high enough to just allow you in. Finally a quick course correction and go with the flow around the protruding boulders.

Boofing the blind drop helps, as you avoid slowing your progress by jumping the frothiness. All goes smoothly, but we wait anxiously, worried about each other until we are all through. Straightforward enough once you've done it.

Nice one Nick.

Below the final log jam and fall

Pleased to survive the crux, we rounded a few more corners to find a beaver dam of huge logs, another portage! This guarded the entrance to the final large fall.

We are happy now as you could see the bridge at the end of the gorge. So a portage over, under and through the log jam, the final few drops and then we have to carry the kayaks up a 100 m scree slope up to the road.

A great tick for me, this has been in the back of my mind since my first outing to the Alps, six years previously. I felt so pleased to have achieved this goal.

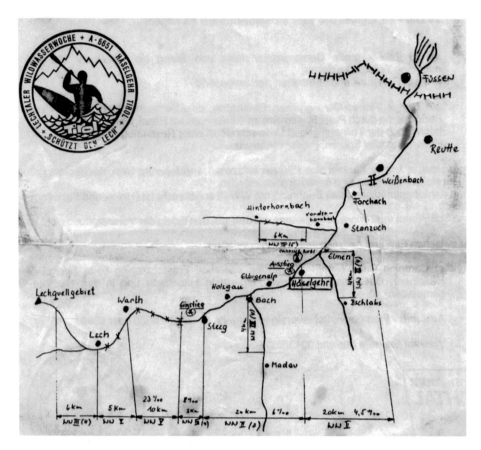

Lech river map

166

Into the Unknown
Maha Kali (December 1992)
John Hough, Chris Dickinson

I first met Chris Dickinson when we were both punters on an organised trip down the Sun Kosi and Trisuli in December 1988. He rang me with an invitation to his house in Ardentinny for the weekend to discuss a project. I jumped at the chance. John Hough, with whom I had worked at an outdoor centre in the Lake District, was also invited.

Apparently, Chris remembered a conversation we had had on the Sun Kosi about other Nepalese rivers that we might attempt. His idea is to explore the Maha Kali. I had never heard of it. Running down the western border of Nepal with India, the Maha Kali drains the western side of Nepal and its tributaries, the East side of the Uttarakhand region of India. Old trade routes existed with trails along the river banks into China. However, the Indians were constructing a new road on the west side of the river. The main reason for the road construction was the close proximity of the Tibetan, and so the Chinese border. This placed the Maha Kali valley within the so-called 'inner line' and so out of bounds for westerners. The track on the Nepalese side in Sudurpaschim province remained a rugged footpath but without the same restrictions. We had gleaned faint rumours that some Indians had rafted from Askot to the new dam near Tanakpur.

Getting there: The plan was to fly to the remote Gokule airstrip and trek to the river over a high pass before heading upriver on the Nepalese bank. We would go as far as time and terrain would allow before descending the river to begin paddling. Straightforward it would seem.

Plans laid and monies paid, John even managed to find some relatively cheap flights on Biman (Bangladesh Airlines). Chris had contacts in Nepal who would sort out the logistics of it all. Chris had some mountain bats which he offered to rent to us!

The plan was complex having several stages but easy to achieve. When John and I arrived on time at Euston and were whisked with ease on the tube to Heathrow terminal 3 at 12.00, we were more than pleased with our prospects.

Chris arrived a short time later but we were unable to check in as John didn't have the tickets. He had arranged to meet a man from the company (now no longer trading) from whom he had bought the tickets. No tickets and no man! A phone call found the individual concerned, who then rushed to the airport by 1 o'clock. Crisis 1 resolved. It was now 14th December. However, our tickets had only been issued on the 13th, which was strange as John had paid for them at the end of August. Smelling a rat, we persuaded the man to remain until we were booked on. As we feared our tickets were stand-by only. So we were told that we could only be issued seats when all other passengers were booked in, and only then if there was space available. Eight months of work and the chance to paddle a virgin river seemed to evaporate before our eyes. We were discussing the relative merits of hanging or drowning our ticket provider when at 3.00 p.m. he rushed over and gave us our boarding passes and seat numbers; crisis 2 sorted. All we had to do was board the plane and we were off.

High pressure over the S.E. England had brought fog, thick fog which decided not to clear. Since we only had standby tickets the Biman officials refused to put us up in a hotel for the night. We had to hire a car and drive 40 miles or so to Tonbridge where Chris's sister put us up for the night, returning at 9.00 a.m. the following morning. So 24 hours later we were still sitting in the airport. The delay could curtail our trip since we had a tight schedule and were meant to fly out from Kathmandu on 16th, Monday afternoon. The delay could bring our whole trip to a standstill even if we did get to Nepal. The day passed with us sat waiting for Biman airline staff to tell us what was happening. We also took turns in watching the departures board as a BA representative had told us that we were more likely to get information from that. Our plane had landed in Paris and so, when the fog partly cleared, it safely made the short hop to Heathrow.

Biman only had a few flights a week, one of these on Saturday and one on Sunday, both to Dacca in Bangladesh. At 3:00 p.m., the departure board flashed boarding at gate 54. We were first to see it and ran for the gate getting near the front of the queue. As we passed through the check-in gate our seat numbers were torn up and we were told to sit wherever there is a space. Since the flight was delayed, there were two lots of passengers trying to get on one plane, two people for every seat. The fact that one set of passengers had already waited 24 hours didn't seem to matter and so a maul ensued. The three of us with oversized hand luggage managed to block the route to a side door. We had noticed our plane on the runway and we were to be transported by bus to it. The door opened and was propelled by the force of the throng behind. Protected by our rucksacks, we made the plane and secured our seats. Crisis 3 endured.

As we landed in Dacca the new day was dawning, but, of course, we had missed our onward flight to Kathmandu, other passengers had missed their connections to Bangkok, Singapore etc.

The check-in desk at Dacca was a sorry place to be. Flights delayed from other European cities had left many passengers trying to reserve seats on flights. The desk was only 10 m long with a small office behind it. The system they adopted was so typical of the third world. After giving in your passport, you felt stranded and without proof of identity, vulnerable to the officials who you just couldn't be sure of. Also, You gave in g your book of tickets (including return tickets) which were placed in your passport and placed amongst piles of other passports. Now we had no proof of your ability to get home. We were told to come back at 14.30, *'Can't we have our boarding passes now'*, *'no'* was the reply *'There's no problem'* - now where had I heard that before? *'Will we get a seat?'* *'No problem.'*

Games of 3-handed bridge helped pass the time but couldn't divert our thoughts. Instead of waiting for our flight to the west of Nepal from Kathmandu, we were sitting in Dacca airport. After a while, one of those budding entrepreneurs appeared, *'Sirs want a tour of Dacca?* We tried to ignore him but he persisted. To humour him Chris inquired how long it would take, *'Only 2 hours sir'*. The banter continued and we were offered a price of 10 dollars each. Chris seemed keen to go as it would pass the day. What if the car broke down etc? I wondered. I said I would wait and get the tickets if the others wanted to go. It seemed to me that there was the potential to make our situation worse by adding another unknown to our unpredictable situation. Then we remembered that we didn't have our passports and so we couldn't leave the airport. Another potential for disaster was thus avoided. I went down to see about our tickets when a local accosted me and tried to persuade me to go and buy him 200 cigarettes from the duty-free shop. Looking around I spotted several security guards all with pistols. *'No, I won't help you.'* After telling him no for the 5th time he gave up. All seemed quiet at the ticket desk and there was no change in the situation.

Then our friendly tour driver appeared again. Obviously, he was having a bad day. '*I get your passports,*' he said. It seemed like a good idea. He rushed behind the ticket desk and talked to a short, balding official. He soon returned saying he could get us a pass out of the airport. I returned to the others, and the tour guide followed. After discussing it with the others, we decided that if he had a mate behind the desk, then maybe he could get our tickets. So we agreed to go on his trip if he could get our passports and boarding passes. He tried, he tried very hard, but did not succeed. A free cup of tea was accompanied by some unappetising '*I wonder where that has been*' snacks, which quickly ended up in the bin. Returning to the top of the stairs at about 2:00 p.m. a sight more reminiscent of the floor of the stock exchange ensued. About 300 people were all squashing forward to try and get their boarding passes for various flights.

Our friendly guide nipped around the back and was told that our flight would not be sorted for at least half an hour. Behind the desk stood three men: the balding chap seemed to be in charge of supervising the other two; a taller chap was making piles and more piles from all the passports; a rather plump guy was trying to quell the crowd. As soon as he offered to talk to someone about 20 people all shouted at him at the same time. In Dutch, English, German, French, Italian, and several other languages that I couldn't make out. The problem was that three flights had been told to board but no one had a boarding pass. Ideally, there were supposed to be three queues: one for Rangoon, one for Delhi and one for Bangkok. They all intermingled as they pushed to the front. The plump man behind the counter went through a wide range of tactics, from going away and having a cup of tea, to '*I'm not talking to any of you.*' The fan above him whooshed around, cooling his head but the crowd became more agitated. A Dutchman, who seemed two metres tall, towered above the throng. Even though he was seven rows back he shouted 'G*ive me my passport,*' the response from behind the desk came in that peculiar Indian dialect of English '*If you take your passport you won't get a seat.*' The Dutchman insisted. From within the piles on the desk, the plump man pulled out his passport and handed it back. No flight for him then.

A change of tactics followed whereby sweets were offered to placate the agitated travellers. It was all quite amusing watching the stressed-out tourists trying to persuade an equally stressed-out official that he should do his job, when in fact he was, trying and answer questions about flights. Up to ten people argued with the plump man, who considering his situation, remained remarkably calm, if frustrated. The main problem seemed to be a lack of knowledge of how the system worked. By now he had had enough and went to sit down in the office. The manager-type just stood there ignoring everyone. His job was only to supervise. When he re-emerged from the office the shouting intensified. Sitting on the steps above I noticed that the queue on the left, the one for Rangoon, had started to move. The tall chap had sorted the passports, tickets and seats and was issuing them. In ten minutes all that flight had gone and then he was able to focus on our flight. Our group adopted a quiet approach. John and Chris tried to hold some space to reduce our competition at the desk. What a team. Within a few minutes, we were at the desk. But just as John was told that our flight had not been sorted the manager kicked into life and asked which flight we were going on. I replied '*Kathmandu,*' and pointed to our passports. He picked them up and handed them over with our boarding passes and we were away. Crisis 4 diverted.

The wait was stressful, so we were relieved we had left it behind. The unnerving steep descent into Kathmandu is always more exciting than it needs to be.

We were met at the airport by our local travel guides and taken to a quiet hotel in the Thamel region of town. As John and I entered our room, four hairy legs protruded from the sheet.

Giant spider

We stood frozen at the thought of such a large spider in the hotel. Reaching for the split paddle on the back of my rucksack. I pounded the body four or five times, but it had not changed. It was then that I realised that it wasn't a spider after all but the fine ends of a blanket. I felt such a fool but we laughed with relief at our stupidity. Exhausted after our journey the distinctive scents of Kathmandu invaded my nostrils. We had arrived.

During our meal that evening, we learned that Nepali airlines had rescheduled all its flights and that even if we had arrived on time we couldn't have flown out until Thursday. Our relief was soon tempered when we realised that this would reduce our paddling time on the Maha Kali by three days, but we couldn't do anything about it.

I awoke Tuesday morning with a dose of the runs. After visiting the shop to see our local contact, we established that the boats had been sent on ahead and that our team of porters were already camped beside the river. However, it was a one-and-a-half-day walk from the airport to the boats. More paddling time had gone. That afternoon at 4:00 p.m., we were told that we had to pay a visit to see the Minister for Tourism as we were travelling into an area not often frequented by western travellers. This also meant that we had to have a liaison officer with us. After waiting an hour or so, we were told that the minister didn't have time to see us. Instead, we were introduced to Minali, who was to accompany us, as the liaison officer. Not only... did he seem unsuitable for the job, but he did not know the area we were to visit, and he had never been out of Kathmandu before. He clearly had no concept of what kayaking was all about; his slightly rotund figure indicated a lack of fitness. Apparently, it was his turn to be the liaison officer and it was to be his first assignment. Not only did we see him as unnecessary but we had to negotiate a deal with him as to his wages for coming with us. After much hard bargaining, a deal was struck, $250 plus meals. We arranged to meet him at the airport at 6:15 a.m. on Thursday. We sorted out our trekking permits.

Chris, rather undiplomatically informed us that since we had a spare day he had sorted a day trip. We were to go to the Bhote Kosi on Wednesday. It would cost us all $105 plus $5 each for the permit. A great idea but how about consulting with us first?

I'm not at my best at 5 a.m. but a swift breakfast sorted that out. The bumpy road to Sun Kosi bazaar did nothing for my upset stomach, though the sunrise on the Himalayas reminded me how lucky we were to be here.

Chris and John at the start of the Bhote Kosi

172

At 10.30 we arrived at Lartza bridge and donned our dry cagoules. The heat already seemed oppressive. A seal launch, into a pool below a narrow fall and slot of FWD, should have been straightforward. I managed OK but John failed to take into account of the speed and direction of the current. Before even paddling a few strokes he found himself pushed underneath some slightly overhanging rocks, 10 m downstream. You can guess the rest, capsize and an unpleasant swim, were followed by a game of bobbing in the upwelling boils underneath the overhang.

Chris, still on the bank, used his line to pull John and his boat from his predicament. Being unable to pull John against the current, Chris allowed him to float down to where I completed the rescue. I was not at all impressed. I hadn't paddled with John previously. I put it down to a lack of recent practice and a consequence of the events of the previous days. Immediately the river steepened, and grade 4 boulder gardens ran into each other.

John takes a nice slide

Some slightly harder rapids tested our rusty skills but enabled us to become accustomed to paddling Mountain Bats. these were not nearly as comfortable or responsive as my Corsica at home. There seemed to be a slight delay in their turning ability. I recall thinking I had better adjust my paddling style to allow for that.

Chris sneaks by a nasty recirculation

Typical Bhote Kosi drops

We river-scouted all the way taking turns to lead and loop through. Continuous grade 4-5, challenging, but so rewarding, required oodles of concentration, many correcting strokes and produced MOT with 'almost capsized' moments. We soon settled into a routine that promised well for the Maha Kali.

After another cooling session, John bucked up his ideas and we carved and flowed more efficiently, with fewer errors. It proved to be a timely challenge, in terms of getting used to the Mountain Bat, for reading and running on tricky water. Our route to our egress point cleared with only one portage of a rather gnarly-looking class 6 fall. We were off the river at 3:30 p.m. After the long drive back, three tired bears stowed their wet gear in the drying room and crashed out early.

There is no rest for the wicked, so we were up again at 6:15 a.m. to get to the airport at 7 a.m. Rebooking flights was easy, as they seemed to give preference to those paying dollars. Minali was a little late. His poor English and bad breath did little to improve our impression of him. The plane flew over valleys full of early morning mist with the backdrop of the snow-clad Himalayas. The flight path was parallel to these giants; my mind floated around the peaks, vaguely recognising Annapurna and a few others, before heading south to Nepalgunj.

After fighting off thirty or so potential porters, we hired two phut-phuts to take us to our hotel since our final flight wasn't until the following morning. The locals seemed amused by our paddles sticking out of the sides of our diesel-gulping transport. We passed myriads of roadside stalls and carts mostly selling peanuts and onions. The Lonely Planet guide listed only two hotels: the Sneka being the better one, ours is the Batika. Yes, we had a booking for the one that was less recommended. Even at midday, the mosquitoes weren't deterred by the fumes from burning coils. After a quick lunch, I checked through my kit only to find that I had left my paddling boots in our Kathmandu hotel drying room.

Minali accompanied John and me to seek out a replacement. A 10-minute rickshaw ride to the town centre ensued to get some last-minute supplies. The town although crowded, was surprisingly pleasant, with many bright-coloured tailors, food stalls and hundreds of shops that sold pots and pans, onions and peanuts. The locals were as industrious as those in Kathmandu but seemed to have more purpose about them. It was shoe shops that I needed, but after visiting six or so it became apparent that the small Nepalese of the Terai plains don't have size 11 feet. So I settled for a pair of size 9 Hush Puppies for about $7. John and I arranged to meet Minali back at the hotel. Shopping completed we hired a rickshaw to take us back agreeing on the price before we set off.

Chatting away we took little notice of the route. Half an hour later we passed a barrier and then stopped at another. 'Stop!' we shouted as we realised that we were about to be taken into India and we didn't have our passports or a visa. Our rickshaw cyclist pointed to the Hotel Batika just over the border. Oh, there were two hotels with the same name. After a few minutes, we explained that it was the wrong one and instead asked for Hotel Sneka. Our driver seemed to understand and started complaining. He turned around and sneaked us back into Nepal arriving another half-hour later at the hotel. Minali was hungry and wanted to eat, but we were going to wait until later. I cut the toes from the uppers of my new shoes and sewed some straps onto them to make them more secure. Later, Minali complained again and so joined us for a second lunch, eating at the other hotel. In Minali's local dialect, he introduced the manager whom we thought was called Supsunder Lami. In fact, the manager had taken our order for soup and salami.

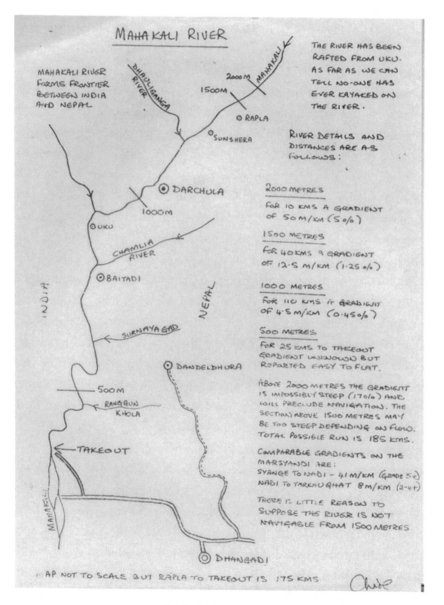

Maha Kali river map

Our taxi didn't arrive on time and after waiting 15 minutes, Minali phoned to find out that it wouldn't be coming at all – some liaison officer! We asked Minali to arrange transport to the airport. He came back with two rickshaws, but we needed 4 to get all our gear on. Another delay. Eventually, we had one each and the race was on. Twenty-five rupees to the airport. One of our rickshaws gained a puncture not far from the airport, where we eventually checked in 20 minutes late. Another crisis averted.

The flight was pleasant if a bit bumpy. All the other passengers were locals except for an American doctor, who lived 6 months in west Nepal and 6 months in the States, trying to raise funds for his surgery in Darchula. He confirmed that he did not know about previous trips on the river. As the plane swung around on the approach to the airstrip at Gokule it flew along the Chamliya river, beautifully blue grade 2–3 and flowing but not in spate. Landing on what was no more than a field, we were pleased to have finally arrived. Our guide Ger, smiled as we emerged from the plane. He was to prove to be much more of a useful liaison officer than our man from the ministry. Our baggage soon disappeared on the backs of Sherpas. As we followed, the plane took off; I suddenly felt a sense of panic as I realised that there was no going back. I was here with two friends and a team of porters that I didn't know. In a strange place, of which I had no knowledge that was more difficult to get to than any place I had been before. I turned to John 'Scary isn't it?' his smile confirmed that he was feeling the same.

As the noise of the plane grew quieter these feelings were soon surpassed by a sense of purpose and determination to get on with the job at hand.

Then the tranquillity of the place became apparent. We strolled over to a small group of tents where we were immediately provided with cups of tea and homemade cake. As we relaxed we chatted over our maps and plans for the next few days. Ger outlined the landscape and route that he had walked the previous week. Our boats were in place, but a 2 day walk away, our schedule allowed one. Another paddling day lost. However, we were here and ready to go. Our adventure had finally begun.

After refreshments, we trekked up and up, and up some more, over 1500 m to an unnamed pass. Endless steep valleys, and peaks of foothills, all were forested, just about as they had been for thousands of years. After about 40 minutes, we stopped for a rest. Minali was struggling. He announced that he wasn't going on unless we paid him another $100 and if we didn't pay the expedition was over. After a few minutes of chat, Chris explained to him that he had signed a contract. We did not intend to pay him anything more.

Minali insisted. When it was made clear that his presence was unnecessary as far as we were concerned, and that we didn't mind if he went back alone, Minali then desisted. We continued over the pass and down, for hours and hours. We trekked through villages and woodland until we got our first peek of our river at Dattu. The water level looked just perfect, not too high, not too low. Ten kilometres upstream near Dhaulakot, we met the porters and our cook, where we made camp just outside the village.

Maha Kali team
Front row Ger, Jon, Chris, Myself, Minali

Since the Maha Kali had never been paddled before, we were keen to get an eye on the first day's paddle.

Early morning fog obscures our first view of our Day 1 gorge

178

A very early start saw us climb up high above the river level and then traverse 600 m above the river. Set at the bottom of a steep V-shaped valley, the early morning temperature was ever so beautiful but hid all below, resisting our attempts at viewing the river; filling the valley with fog.

A few hours later, the fog relented. We were encouraged, even excited by what we saw. However, this was only one section. We were not naive enough to think it might be like this all the way. Three hours later, we had to avoid long trains of goats on the single track. During one of which almost overbalanced Chris down the slope, as he filmed. Eventually, we arrived at the kayak's location, which was, disappointingly, still 400m above the river. Ger had decided that he was not sure where we wanted to begin, so he had kept his options open. After all our lost days we only had about 7 days and a long way to go, exploring an unknown river. Would there be sufficient time? 7 km further upstream from Dhaulakot the river flowed out of an almost vertical-sided valley, with a continuous white line of steep unknown rapids.

First view down into the initial river section on the hike in

Our upstream limit of exploration was decided. The whole team, Sherpas, cooks and even Minali helped us get our kayaks down to the river at 1300 m altitude. Just after 9:00 a.m., we departed into the unknown, where no one had ever been.

We adopted the looping system as a way of sharing the lead, sharing the exploration, and scouting. We provided safety cover whilst taking photos. To begin, the rapids were grade 3, but very soon grade 4 drops interspersed flatter pools. At times the grade 4 fused together, then more often, until that became the norm. Inspection became more frequent, but everything had paddle-able lines. Danger lurked in almost every rapid, boulder chokes were common, and ledges and chutes became common. This was so much better than we could have dreamed of.

After a few hours, we noticed people, then diggers and bulldozers about 300 m up onto the Indian side of the gorge.

First rapids just around the bend from the start

Many loose boulders were being pushed over the cliffs, fortunately not reaching the river. This was a new road being built by the Indian Government, up to China, to increase trade in the area. We noticed soldiers with rifles, which reminded us that we did not have permits to be on the right Indian bank, only the left, Nepalese bank. In fact, the border lay down the middle of the river.

We worked well as a team. The character of the river was consistent, enabling us to relax. Then the river narrowed slightly, leading to 3 ledges in quick succession, each holding a wide river-wide stopper, each at a slight angle to the flow. It was my turn to lead, the ledges looked OK-ish, I was probe, hitting each stopper at right angles and used my momentum to punch each one - super! Chris followed.

Chris follows down one of the longer steeper sections

John made the first, got slightly turned by the second, so was consequently off-line and gets gobbled by the third. He tried to roll, twice. The Scrimbly won. Thoughts flashed through my head, OMG, we were so remote, we had a swimmer. I glanced at Chris, '*I'll get John*' Chris shouted, as he ferried into the flow and assisted John's swim to the right bank. His kayak was less cooperative and decided to follow the main flow, down the class 4 chaos. There is little choice, I had to follow, read and run, adrenaline honing my senses. We can't lose a kayak on day one! That would be the expedition over. Our first descent ended. One hundred and fifty metres later, I caught and got ahead of John's Mountain Bat, and flipped it upright before managing to nudge it onto a midstream boulder. Somehow, I scrambled up onto the same boulder, no more than two metres long and a metre wide, holding two kayaks and a paddle, and then waited.

A few minutes later, Chris with John carrying his paddle appeared with a throw line. Soon, John was reunited with his kayak and I had joined them as illegal immigrants in India.

At lunch, it was time to take stock and review. It was just a simple misjudgement by John. We decided Hobson had won, we can only continue. Not far downstream on the left, the Nepali bank was now a 150 m vertical cliff. With the river looking steeper, we thought we had better inspect. Just around the corner, literally 80 m below that mid-stream boulder where I had just sat, the whole river sumped under boulders. Certain death. If I had not stopped John's boat it would have been lost. If I had paddled two more drops I would be no more. But this was not a time to dwell. Our antics had been seen from above.

Soon, our lunch is interrupted as children appeared, as if from the rocks. They had seen us and scrambled down the steep-sided valley from the road. We had no Indian visa. Before our trip, we had been refused permits to go up the Indian side of the river. The number of children had grown to 40 who were joined by a few adults. It was only a matter of time before the armed soldiers might join them.

We had to move fast, to do the portage. Thinking quickly, we grabbed our paddles, called the locals over and motioned to them to carry our kayaks. Soon they understood and obliged, and so we hurried rather rapidly over and around huge boulders. In 10 minutes we had portaged 400 m past the boulder-choked sump.

The local lads help with the portage.

Swiftly, we paddled off, away from the soldiers, my mind was full of what had just occurred. Would the next stretch bring more of the same, more close shaves? But it was time to focus, we were more cautious now, the rapids eased slightly and we made good progress without incident. After 6 km, we arrived at the confluence with the Indian tributary of Dhauliganga, where the flow increased by 40%. The river was pushier and required some bold leads. At about

5:00 p.m., the river headed in a more southerly direction. The difficulty increased. The drops became bigger, more, congested, and closer to grade 5-6.

It was about an hour or so to dusk, and mentally exhausted by the constant stress of route finding, and physically tired, we decided to stop. Downstream the possibilities of paddling looked limited. It would take a very long time to inspect and sort the safety cover. From here on, it would be different, requiring more caution, and setting safety would be required on almost every drop. We had just enough emergency kit and food to stay out one night if we needed. But the big picture, with our now limited time to complete our journey, offered a difficult choice.

The start of the 3 km section that stopped our progress

Unsure of our exact position, we estimated a few km to where we had aimed to egress for the day, where we hoped to meet our team. Chris volunteered to follow a goat track across scree slopes to find our camp.

Meanwhile, in case Chris was unsuccessful, John and I started to carry the kayaks, one at a time between two, up scree, over boulders, and through scrubby vegetation. With three kayaks, and only two tired people we made slow progress. After what seemed hours, we had moved the kayaks up 60 m and along about 300 m. Fortunately, 90 min after he left, Chris arrived with 3 porters. The goat track had persisted, leading him directly to our Sherpas and camp. Hugs of relief! Now, 2 per boat we should make better progress in the growing gloom. But no, headbands out, the Sherpas each mounted a Mountain Bat on their back. They went, fast, so unbelievably fast, that we could not keep up. We used paddles for balance along the narrow track, across steep-sloped terrain. They had flip-flops,

I had my toeless Hush Puppies, and Chris and John were in their wetsuit boots. But we didn't keep up. After an hour, it was almost dark, we caught them up where the track meandered between small cliffs, one of which deposited a falling rock onto a Sherpa's head, cutting it badly. Using my first aid kit, I stopped the bleeding, the wound was dressed, and he was off again, we ran to keep up. Thirty minutes later, we were sharing chai in camp.

We were so relieved in so many ways, we had made it to the Nepali confluence with the Kala Gad river. A totally absorbing but engaging day of exploration, the outcome was so good. We felt humbled after such an incredible and impressive carry from the three porters.

The following day, almost every muscle had to be encouraged into action. We had a river to run, covering at least 160 km of unknown territory, with just 6 days to complete the challenge.

Below the Kala Gad confluence, the river gradient lessened slightly, still technical rocky rapids with bigger ledges but with some longer pools between the rapids. The boulders were probably larger, but more rounded, with more choice of lines, more defined eddy lines. The difficulty remained between class 3 and 5 all the way to Dharchula. The day went very well, with only one portage. Everything flowed nicely. The occasional inspection was conducive to filming, but again we deemed safety best done from kayaks on the river. Probing proved a little more necky than following.

Chris takes a typical rapid downstream from Dattu

At Dharchula, 300 or so people stood on the suspension bridge and waved as we navigated the more than 1 km long rapid over which the bridge stood. We thought we might be the cause of a disaster, with so many locals leaning over the very precarious suspension bridge structure.

Christmas Eve evening was spent with many uninvited visitors from the nearest village, surrounded by locals, who sat just 3m from us watching every move. It felt unnerving being the animals in the zoo. Fortunately, we were soon removed from their gaze, as Ger had negotiated the use of a room in a local hut, where we could keep warmer, eat dinner and smile as we danced to the rhythm of drums with our team.

Christmas Day. The road no longer followed the river. We said goodbye to our team, as we anticipated covering longer distances, and moving more quickly. Having packed our sleeping bags, a set of spare clothes, 2 stoves and food for 3 days in the back of our kayaks, we were off on our own, 145 km to go.

Christmas Cracker rapids

We started a bit later, thus allowing the air to warm up. We paddled more continuous grades 3 and 4 with some steeper drops. Two hours after departure, we shared lunch by a huge boulder at the top of a long rapid. A long, long rapid full of ledges and huge boulders, class 5. Despite the difficulties, we all had good runs and named it 'Christmas Cracker'.

Chris getting into 'Christmas Cracker'

More of the same brought us to Jolijibi to the confluence of the Goriganga. The river now flowed southwards, and the water volume has doubled, but the altitude was/ now only 800 m so it would be warmer. After the confluence, the river significantly changed its nature with much longer, flatter but flowing sections. We made camp soon after the confluence, disappointed that the fantastic challenging rapids had not continued but at the same time relieved that the major difficulties seemed to be over. The river valley is now wider, and more mature, though still in a wide gorge, with ridgetops towering out of sight.

The river was less steep now, but still flowing with longer easier sections of classes 1 and 2 with the occasional 3. Small crags dominate the scenery. A small trekking path left the river at the confluence with the Chamliya. 5 km further on, at Jhulaghat the river squeezed through a 5 m gap, the water almost still. Here was the last bridge for 100 km.

Chris pinned in the wave

The river course follows long bends. So it was with some surprise that we hear a rumbling ahead and encountered large boulders. Soon we are in the midst of a long wave train. Class 3+ but with exploding standing waves. Our progress halted as we played for a while.

Chilling time

Then disaster, as Chris was surfing on a breaking wave. He suddenly stopped, how could that be?

Chris was pinned on a pointed boulder, hidden just under the surface in one of the waves. MOT, it was a few anxious seconds before he is thrown free. This is no place for a disaster. It would take days to get help.

Downstream the river becomes jungle-fringed, with pristine sandy beaches and almost no population. Monkeys and the rich diversity of birdlife would make this an ornithologist's dream. Occasionally, a lone villager, scraped the shingle bank, presumably for some mineral or other.

About 1km further on, we heard more rumbling. Chris suggested that he goes first and take some video footage. He bounces down the wave train, broke out three-quarters of the way down and gave us the thumbs up. John and I decided to run the wave train almost together, *I lead, unable to see over the large waves, trying to go over the peaks of each wave. Then almost sideways, the third wave down seems not to have an exit. It's a huge hole. I fall in sideways, despite the excessive edge of my kayak. I almost capsized. I lean into the breaking wave wall and brace my paddle in the wave. I disappear, and then my boat comes up vertically to be thrown over the back of the stopper wall. I capsize, but surface from the downstream side and roll.*

What the f***! I turned around and saw John heading directly downstream into the jaws> He back looped as well, but got sucked back into the hole, and rolled over sideways, before fortunately being released from the far side. Completely disoriented, John swam As I nudge his boat to the side, he swam alongside it.

An argument ensued. How could Chris let us paddle into that hole? It was not somewhere I would send my worst enemy. Chris seems to think it's funny. Having swum unnecessarily, John was fuming and it didn't help when Chris blurted out '*It will look good on the video*' then he added '*You are OK so what's the problem?*' I couldn't reconcile his decision to not inform us. The idea of the probe is to let the group know about potential problems. This was a crucial part of team paddling. Could we trust Chris again? The river eases, and so stress levels fall. We float where no one has been before.

Soon after, we reached the confluence with the Surnaya Gad where we camped. There were no trails here, it was so isolated. We covered about 40 km today. As we cooked rice and veg for dinner 5 sets of legs hurriedly walked past, no heads. The top half of their bodies disappeared inside 1.5 m high piles of freshly cut grass. John said '*Hello*' so they fled as if in terror.

It reminded me of some tales in Richard Bangs' excellent River Gods book, '*Strangers in strange objects floated by.*' Our presence was a total surprise to them. Even in their wildest imagination, they would not they expect to see the likes of us. In this remote place, it is possible these locals had no knowledge about kayakers and perhaps, not even seen foreigners.

Local bringing the day's harvest scurry away from us

Author on the river Gods' seat at our last camp

We were tired after the long day on the river. The tension was still high after the afternoon's incident. Following dinner, John went to bury onion skins and orange peel. Chris objected, saying it was pristine wilderness so we should pack everything out. John maintained that burying the biodegradable vegetable scraps was OK. Secretly, I concurred with John, but for the sake of avoiding a 2 versus 1 argument in a small team, I tried to agree with both.

The disagreement seemed surreal, it was a release of tension but at such odds with where we were, the goals we had set, detracting from what we had achieved as a team.

Chris was determined to have his way.

In the discussion that followed, hints emerged that Chris considered it was his expedition to which we were invited. It was intimated that we were, in effect, punters as he had provided the kayaks and sorted the logistics. I recall John and I offered to help sort logistics when we met to discuss plans months before our trip. However, Chris declined our offer, telling us this was not necessary. It also explained why we had not been consulted when Chris decided to go to the Bhote Kosi. Later, chatting with John, we considered again how Chris had deliberately sent us into that hole for 'his video'.

Near the end of the Chure gorge

The following morning we floated through more jungle-like vegetation. Floating past, we observed many species of birds, I deemed this was an ornithological paradise. Occasional grade 2 or 3 rapids improved the white-water interest. We saw no one. At a 2 km long but definite bend, the river changed direction from south to west into the Chure gorge. The hills rose as we entered a sandstone gorge. What delights did it hold? Well, to be honest, only delights of scenery and riffle rapids. We made camp on another even more isolated beach in the gorge, surrounded by cliffs on all sides.

The sun set early. Chilly air just after dawn brought misty fog hanging over the river, which was kind of spooky, as we feared it might hide a surprise sinister gorge. The thought of Scrimblies was in our heads. However, the river flowed swiftly but peacefully until after a few hours. About noon the fog started to lift, just before we emerged from the gorge, the fog cleared, revealing a hot sunny day.

As the morning passed, the gradient increased a little, bringing more swift-flowing flattish water interspersed with long shingle bed rapids consisting of three wave trains.

Within a few minutes, the Chure hills were far behind as we drifted across the plains of the Terai. The river channel became braided. You may recall we had no visa to enter India, so after a while, we wondered where the border was.

After delaying our decision for far too long, we saw a lake in the distance. We guessed this was the dam water of the now-growing Tanakpur hydroelectric project. It indicated we had gone too far.

John in class 3 braided section

We turned and pulled our kayaks back upstream for 3 km. I noticed a cairn only 1 m high, this was the border we guessed. This was so vague, we wondered why the locals might even adhere to the border.

Chris strolled over into a woodland nearby, returning a few minutes later with a lot of villagers who helped carry our kit into the village. This was a different sort of place; the end of our trip? not quite! It took all our time to keep an eye on our kit, which we put in a pile for fear it might just disappear. The villagers were friendly enough and offered us local green tea. Our team of porters were meant to meet us in this village, but of them, there were no signs. Maybe it was another village? This was our last scheduled day on the river. We were due to catch a bus from Mahendranagar to Nepalgunj that evening. The only problem, we anticipated was that Mahendranagar was 25 km away and we had 3 kayaks with paddling kits. After some negotiations using non-common languages, we persuaded some of the villagers to help us. They were not interested in dollars and we had very little Nepalese currency.

A motley crew set off; with one kayak strapped to an old bicycle that had one flat tyre, one kayak between 4 children and some older guys. After a few minutes, a few kids ran on ahead, leaving the kayak, which we added to our burden of bulging dry bags and paddles. As soon the path became bouldery where we crossed a small, almost dry stream bed, the bicycle porter had had enough. Unstrapping the kayak, and abandoning it, he just turned around and rode back towards the village. Now we were left with us and just 3 older gents.

What to do? Did I hear bugles? You know about the cavalry from the old Wild West films? Just in our hour of need, our team of Sherpas appeared. It seems they were driving over from Jhulaghat when the road became blocked with snow. They spent almost a day digging a way through to get to us.

The walk became long. The hike was hot, with not much water to drink. So many trails going nowhere. Eventually, we came into an area of endless irrigated fields. The way was obscure, but Ger seemed to have a sixth sense. Even though amazingly, each kayak was carried by one porter, we had to jog to keep up. Four hours later, we sat at the bus station sipping cold Coke Cola.

We took the early evening bus, arriving in Nepalgunj after dark. The following day was New Year's Eve. I was so looking forward to a few beers and a comfortable bed. Our flight to Kathmandu was cancelled, so another bus, overnight this time. Our kit was safely secured on the roof. Somehow, I was unlucky enough to get the seat by the door, which didn't close properly. We 'celebrated' the new year, freezing overnight on a very cold, bumpy, sleepless bus ride, my sleeping bag secured on the roof.

Just after daybreak, we embarked on the long road climb before descending to Kathmandu. Swerving around broken trucks, being fixed on the tarmac of the main road, where they had stopped. Our bus halted at about 6:30 a.m.

The locals disembarked to take advantage of dhal and rice at the roadside shack. We decided not to bother. It turned out that it was a fortunate choice. Just to the side of the shack was a murky puddle a few centimetres deep. A guy splashed some water onto his face before cleaning his teeth and spitting the froth into the puddle. A dog lapped up some cool liquid, before urinating close by, close enough for the trickle to join the puddle.

The influx of customers induced a young lad to come out with a big pile of stainless-steel plates which he washed, in the same dirty puddle. I expect the dhal was extra tasty. We had but one day in Kathmandu, before flying home. Having had so many problems with our tickets on the way out, we found ourselves visiting a local travel agent. On our behalf, he rang Biman airlines, only to find out that our intended flight was overbooked. On our behalf, he secured new flights, to London via Delhi with an overnight stop in transit at the airport as we had no visa to enter India. At least the food on Thai air was much superior to Biman. It transpired that Chris was intending to make a video of 'his' expedition. That was cool. However, if we wanted a copy, we would have to pay for our share of his new video camera and waterproof video housing!

It had been a fantastic trip. We had been pushed to and almost past our limits. Adventure achieved, misadventure avoided, just! We had overcome difficulties right from the start, success brought so much more reward and satisfaction than I expected.

We had completed the first descent, almost 200 km of the Maha Kali River, in kayaks and no one could take that away from us. We were proud but a slightly divided team.

Bringing it all Together

Sikkim, Stepping Up (December 1993)

Sten Sture, Dave Hansen, Richard Evans, Chris Walker, Gareth Walker, George Novak

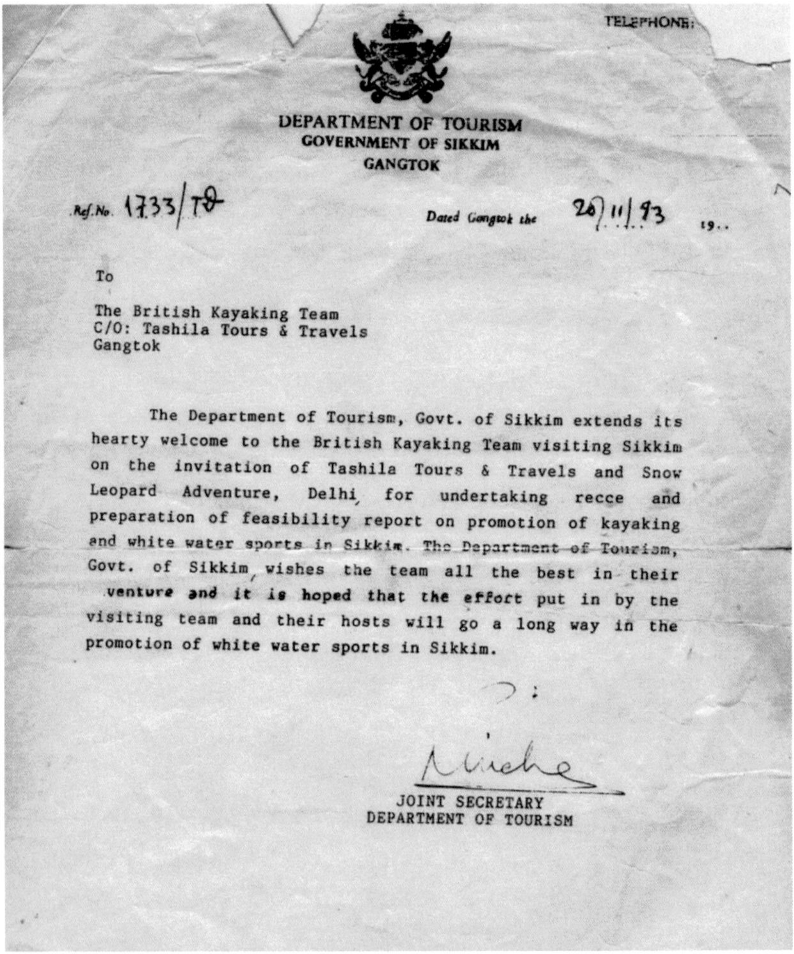

TELEPHONE:

DEPARTMENT OF TOURISM
GOVERNMENT OF SIKKIM
GANGTOK

Ref. No. 1733/78

Dated Gangtok the 26/11/93   19..

To

The British Kayaking Team
C/O: Tashila Tours & Travels
Gangtok

    The Department of Tourism, Govt. of Sikkim extends its hearty welcome to the British Kayaking Team visiting Sikkim on the invitation of Tashila Tours & Travels and Snow Leopard Adventure, Delhi, for undertaking recce and preparation of feasibility report on promotion of kayaking and white water sports in Sikkim. The Department of Tourism, Govt. of Sikkim, wishes the team all the best in their venture and it is hoped that the effort put in by the visiting team and their hosts will go a long way in the promotion of white water sports in Sikkim.

JOINT SECRETARY
DEPARTMENT OF TOURISM

Our letter of invitation

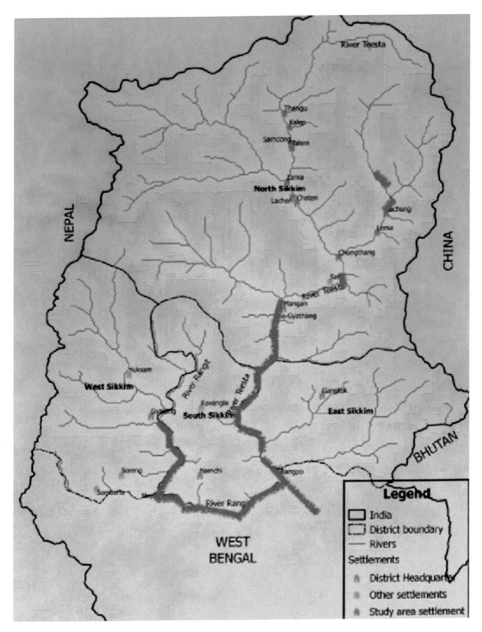

Map of Sikkim. Pink highlights indicate the sections we paddled

After the success of the Maha Khali trip with its thrills and emotions, ups and downs, I decided to look for something similar. Almost all the larger rivers in Nepal have been run. While looking at a map of Northern India, I noticed the tiny kingdom of Sikkim.

After contacting two rafting companies in Delhi, I received a positive response from Ajeet Baja of 'Snow Leopard'. He had done some rafting in the area and had kayaks to hire. He was also coming to a Travel Expo in Manchester, so we would be able to meet and discuss plans. Soon after that, Ajeet informed us that he had managed to get us a permit to paddle in Sikkim. Even better, the Sikkim Tourist board had agreed to support our trip by providing transport and some accommodation on the way. My application for sponsorship to Malden Mills in the USA was successful.

Having asked around my group of paddling mates, I soon had a team of willing participants. Chris had done a short interview with the Westmorland Gazette *'It's going to be choppy'* was their interpretation.

However, it was only 2 days before our flights, that our booty arrived, purple Polartec fleece tops for all.

16th December

We were met at Bagdogra airport by Ajeet and his team to be whisked off to a local hotel before on the 17th moving across the hot plains of Northern India. Stopping at a bridge on which monkeys paraded, the river was a wide shallow affair. Ajeet announced that winter had come early in the mountains, and the snowmelt had finished so water levels were very low. Our plans were dashed. Well no! We all burst out laughing, this was a wind-up. We still had 2 hours to get to Sikkim. The joke broke the ice and somehow brought us all together as a team.

Not really knowing what to expect from the rivers, we resolved to look and see what we might find, take it in sections and paddle what we could without taking undue risks. We had no spare kayak.

Since Sikkim is an autonomous region of India, Ajeet had arranged special permits for us to enter and kayak. We had to get our passport stamped once at the border and again on the bridge near Teesta Bazaar, before arriving at our camp by the confluence of the Teesta and Rangit rivers. The first job was to select our kayaks. As the organiser, the others kindly suggested I could have the first pick, so the Corsica for me – same as I had at home. The kayak selection was largely determined by who could fit into what. Some were less happy than others with their choice. But still, a day of active paddling would see us practised and sorted.

17ᵗʰ December

The following day we headed off downstream on the Teesta for a warm-up, 20 km to Kalijohra, class 3 pool drop rapids, some were a little pushier. Worryingly George swam a few times, but still smiling he informed us he was just out of practice. Sunny, and warm with a jungle-like forest and flocks of red parrots, this certainly was a kind of different paddling experience. Ajeet had done a spectacular job, tapping up the Ministry of Tourism. They were so keen for us to come to explore they provided us with a bus for the duration of the trip.

Where to next?

18ᵗʰ December

Today found us driving upstream almost to Rangpo, where we paddled 4 hours back to our camp at the confluence. The river was very similar to the previous day but a little steeper and so faster, with a few longer rapid sections and no swims. The Sikkim tourist board had invited us to Darjeeling. The narrow roads were not the best, so the bus banger, Sanjay, was gamely employed. Apparently, if he was banging it was OK to pass other vehicles. So we worried a lot when he desisted. At Darjeeling, the Himalayan Mountaineering Institute, Colonel Dut of the Indian Army officiated at a passing out ceremony for the Sherpa mountain guides. We were the invited guests. The Colonel became most interested in our expedition, asking if we were going on after, to explore some rivers, which we had never heard of, in Assam.

19th December

The morning found us driving 5 hours up the Rangit river, to the Pemayangste Monastery above Legship. We eventually arrived in the dark at the Elgin Mount Padim Hotel a rather posh affair perched on a hilltop. All courtesy of the tourist board. Come morning I got out of bed and pulled back the curtains. WOW! Since we arrived after dark, I was not even aware, but looking up, filling the view, Kanchenjunga in all its glory. The world's third-highest peak was plastered with snow catching the saloon pink sunrise on its white slopes and glaciers. Not a bad way to start a day.

Sunrise Kanchenjunga

The excursion enabled us to spy out the Rangit river. Upstream from Legship, 2 km of class 4 or 5 led into an unpaddleable section which in turn joined the outflow from a HEP station. Above the 2 km, hardly any water flowed at all. From Legship it seemed to be class 4 with some 3 and a few gorges that we couldn't see into. Just above Naya Bazaar, the river became easier until it entered a small gorge. Below this, it looked like pool drop rapids.

Ajeet had to return to Delhi to run his business, leaving his assistant Rahul Rao to sort the logistics.

20ᵗʰ December

Keen for more paddling, we drove, 2 km downstream of Legship to the Kalet Chu confluence. The river proved challenging, mostly bouldery rapids surrounded by jungle. We played our way down class 3, with the occasional gorge lined by cliffs where grade 4 was more common. We even found some hot springs to wallow in. A tougher section at the 2 km Reshi gorge hid a class 5 affair where boulders forced a couple of rolls.

Some powerful holes saw Dave do a back ender and Gareth roll again. George had two swims, but despite his bravado, seems to be losing his confidence. We finished about 1 km upstream from Naya Bazaar. Cook Nakul provided us with strange but tasty treats; potato pakora, dosa-thin crispy pancake with Rasgolla – sweet curd, being typical.

The 'blob' at the confluence of the Rangit and Ramman rivers

The team was ready to go

21st December

At 9:15 a.m., we found ourselves at Jorethang, where the Ramman river confluence flowed into the Rangit at 90°, creating a strange river feature – the blob. The top of the blob was half a metre above the river level on all sides. With enough speed, you could paddle on top, to be flummoxed by the upwelling water. Each side was like a stopper; surviving became a mystery skill, which we all mastered with practice. Downstream, the river proved challenging, with mostly bouldery rapids surrounded by jungle. The paddling was slightly easier than the previous day with more shingly rapids. Flocks of red parrots flew above and monkeys howled as we passed. There was more time to admire the scenery, and a few holes to trap us. George rolled twice in one rapid. That night 4 jackals visited the camp, to be chased off by George who was out for a midnight wee.

It was time to move north to the headwaters of the Teesta. A long drive north through many Temi tea-growing terraces. Glimpses into the valley bottom teased us with Kanchenjunga majestic above. The day ended in Gangtok where we spent the night at the Mayur hotel, again free of charge.

One of the few views in the Teesta River from our drive northwards

At Gangtok, it took 75 minutes to get some traveller's cheques exchanged for cash and Dave acquired provisions for the following week.

Further north of Phodong was another police checkpoint, where our passports and permits were checked. Despite myself having stomach pains, and Sten flu-like symptoms, the occasional view into the river saw suitably challenging rapids and increased our excitement. At Mangang, George was accosted by a man who insisted on him wearing a large snake like a scarf. We found weevils in a chocolate cake that we had just purchased. Just upstream from Mangang the Teesta valley heads NW to Dzongu, but our permit forbade us to cross the bridge. So instead, we followed the Lachung Chu River to the East, onto Tung, the river far below in a deep gorge. Odd glimpses looked like class 4 or foaming white death. At Tung, the river crossing was another police checkpoint. The river was a steep 4-5 with fantastic blue water. We removed on to Chungthang, the river below was more powerful and very steep. The road was recently blasted through cliffs; large boulders that still lay embedded in the new tarmac were a cause for concern.

The team in the Lachung valley, in our purple Polartec tops

Our permits forbade us to travel up the Lachen Chu river above Chungthang as the Chinese border was not so far, and foreigners were barred. This was almost fortunate for the parts of the river that we could see were big waterfalls or class 5 and 6. At least we didn't have the option of making that decision. Our option was to follow the valley of the Lachung Chu. It too was very steep and had lots of waterfalls with some class 5 sections. Twenty-four kilometres of hairpins found us at a hostel in Lachung. After dinner, we were provided with chang, an alcoholic potion made by rinsing boiling water through germinating highland barley. It's a kind of wine with very low alcohol content which tastes solvent-like. Chris took a big swig and almost fainted. We were at 2700 m altitude and had ascended quickly; it was most likely that he was light-headed due to the altitude. Sten had a fever, and Richard had an ailment of stomach cramps and diarrhoea. Gareth was coughing like a steam train.

22nd December

After heating the bus diesel tank with a stove to unfreeze it, we headed higher. Outside Lachung, whilst we spent an hour waiting at another checkpoint, we decided to have a 100 m race and then spent 10 minutes recovering from the effort. Still, it was sunny. 23 km later we arrived at Yumthang, the valley of the flowers, at 3500 m altitude. The air was so cold despite the bright sun. The water was blue, but so cold since it was glacier melt. The Lachung Chu was shallow, but we couldn't resist the opportunity. We floated a few kilometres below Chombu, 6362 m on grade 2 water, trying to avoid getting our hands wet in the icy water.

Lachung Chu 3500 m

Setting off at 3500m on the Lachung Chu

At our egress, was a fine surprise. A bridge led to a building, inside which hot springs were to be found. A hot, sulphurous bath, at 3500 m altitude was an unexpected treat. Downstream from here, the river was class 4 and 5, with the possibility of paddling, but with such cold water, altitude and the paddleable sections being interspersed with many boulder chokes, discretion won over valour. The volume increased rapidly as meltwater joined the main flow from the peaks above.

Part of the section we paddled above Lachung

The Lachung stretch

Lachung Chu

Below Lachung – getting tastier

23rd December

Above Lachung, the river seemed possible but held steep rapids between high boulders. The altitude and cold contrived against us. This persuaded us to decline again. However a few km above the bridge at Lachung the gradient eased slightly, the boulders slightly more spaced apart, until we were unable to resist.

Boulder chokes

Soon after setting off the winter sun emerged. The water was blue and there were many boulders, making continuous class 4. After inspecting we try and remember safe lines so that all becomes possible. The fast-flowing steep river was just so cool to paddle. We inspected next to a huge boulder and portage 100 m, after which the gradient increased. We ran it sort of blind, class 4 all the way, superb. A lovely long slide rapid was the pick of the bunch. Some classy stuff here.

Occasionally, we took turns to set safety up, but it was never needed. Absorbed by the river, the situation, the remoteness, no one wanted a mistake. Some fine leads and good teamwork saw us through.

It was quite a long portage back to the road where the bus awaited. It was just 5 km, but a sweet first descent, in such a location; so worthwhile. After a few kilometres, the river turned right and heads off over through steeper boulders, then ever more complex falls. It is too much for us, too much for anyone?

The gorge above Chungtang

Below this, the river enters a deep gorge of falls and unrunnable grade 5, 6, and X terrain. Some of the falls looked possible, but all together, the effort-reward conundrum was not conducive enough to persuade us. Just too hard. all too remote, even though we could see down into most of the river. I would take days to complete the section. A large portion would require portaging. It was just so tempting, but a day will be needed for just a few kilometres, time is not on our side, surely there were more rewarding sections downstream? From Chungtang down we inspect it a few times but decided it is not for us.

24th December

We drove downstream to Tung but are delayed 2 hours at roadworks. After reaching the Tung police checkpoint, we were told the bus was oversize and we wouldn't be allowed back up today. So we walked up the river's left bank and inspected a few kilometres. That evening Richard was now very ill so we decided to give him one of the two courses of antibiotics that we had brought with us. It was amusing to see him plead with the first pill '*Please work.*' We bivvied out by the police checkpoint.

25th December

On Christmas day, a cold morning dawned. At 6:00 a.m., as we shared tea, about 50 villagers walked by, each no more than 5' tall, each with a lump hammer. Their day was spent pulverising small boulders on the river bank to make hardcore for new roads.

With the road now open again we drove back upstream to Thong, only Dave and I decided to paddle, the others ill or sensible. They helped us down a steep track to a small bridge. We got on below the bridge and are straight into grade 5 then 4, it all has to be read and run. Fortunately, our inspection the previous day has given us markers: huge riverside boulders, with unique shapes, that mark key places to manoeuvre. After what seems a short run, but maybe 2 km the flow eases to class 2. This is fortunate as the hardest rapid is next, a steep 4 m tongue into turmoil, FWD. The previous day we contemplated this iffy grade 5 drop, but today it looks meaner, too sucky, so we portage.

Dave and I gave each other the thumbs up and reminded each other of the markers. The crux - at that massive flat boulder on the left, we had to go close but not too close, then head right. Grade 4+ again. It all went quiet and blue. I roll so did Dave. It was so fast, bursting a few holes, going right, then hard left, past the marker already! The pace seemed to slow, I had to focus, then ride over a wave, through a hole which broke over my head, then I broke out on the right, and I wait for Dave.

Somewhere in the last rapid above Tung, Xmas day

We were off again, my arms were pumped, I tried to relax my grip, I went right to the crux, burst through and ride that boil line down past the boulder onto a tongue. Then I went through some standing waves, head right, break out. I made it. I had never been this pumped before. We could see the Tung bridge 400 m downstream, just one rapid to go. It is steep. We'd scouted it from the side yesterday. After sharing a Mars bar, Dave and I hold our hands out, both shaking with excitement. We took deep breaths, to calm ourselves down. We knew we needed to be left of the middle to begin. We had plotted a route around boulders to reach this point.

The final rapid today was a very steep, big, powerful boulder choke with most rocks covered. We see the first part is the munchiest. We acknowledged the others on the left bank. They give thumbs up and their throw lines were ready.

Off into the flow, I led, Dave directly behind. The approach goes well, I moved from the far right to the left, cruising to the entry point. Over the lip, I sink up to my armpits but keep paddling. Two more drops required the same. Maybe the first bit wasn't the most tricky. I was totally absorbed, reactive to the flow, bracing on cushions, bursting through holes. The moment was interrupted when I heard a shout from the bank. Looking back, I see Dave had capsized in the second step. There was not much chance to roll, he tried but got sucked out of his kayak. I reached calmer water, still pumped, my forearms screaming. I had to break out as soon as possible. The team deployed a throw line accurately, enabling Dave to grab it the first time. He rolled onto his back, they pendulum him to the bank, they've got Dave secured, phew.

His kayak had another idea, so it took a different route. I considered trying to follow, but the final rapids from my eddy to the bridge are committing. After the bridge, we had seen the river enter a vertical-sided ravine. To enter would be a new expedition of its own - where gorge monsters live. I decided I cannot follow.

We took Christmas lunch outside the police checkpoint. The rock bashers walked past, making us feel guilty, as we had so much. Even so, they plodded by without acknowledging us. That was Dave's trip over in terms of paddling, no kayak, no spare. Having been so elated at Lachung, I now felt a sense of shared glumness in our team.

Having decided to drive around the next 10 km gorge, the hairpins took us high above the gorge 'Keep an eye on the river, you never know.' A few minutes later a shout, someone had seen a yellow flash on the river. As the bus reversed we hoped. There, stuck on the boulder, by a shingle beach, on our side of the gorge, 120 m below, was Dave's kayak.

Grabbing a throw line, but otherwise, without thinking, we charged down a vague track. As we descended very fast, a guy appeared from the deep undergrowth with a machete. What now! There was no way we wanted to fight; no way we could win.

He saw us and bolted downwards to escape us. We followed him down the track to get to the kayak. Apparently, he was illegally cutting timber and thought we might be the authorities trying to arrest him. 10 min later we had descended 120 m to the river. Chris waded in and secured the kayak until we fixed a line and hauled it in. We noticed it was misshapen. Sanjay helped us carry it back up to our bus.

40 minutes later, we were off to Mangan, then Dzongu. The gloominess that hung over the trip was gone. I always find it encouraging when success is plucked from the jaws of despair. As a team, we paddled what we could. We had shared Dave's loss and now his joy. The damage was nothing that some hot boiling water couldn't remould. Even Richard was feeling much better.

Dave's kayak after being retrieved from the river

As I said previously at Dzongu, we weren't allowed to cross the bridge, but as we gazed at the river below, a lady came to chat. She claimed to be the Queen of Sikkim. Maybe it was lost in her translation, as her dress suggested otherwise. However, she did offer us a room to spend the night which we gladly accepted.

26th December

6 hours of paddling today proved to be testing. Dave rolled in the first rapid, a long complex grade 4. We undertook many inspections but ran everything after sussing safe-ish lines. Unfortunately, in one such rapid Chris became

211

momentarily pinned sideways on the rock. This was the start of a bad day for him. After several swims, he decided to walk up to the road. The day passed with over 40 grade 3+ or 4 problems. Lunch was taken at the first X a portage, by a bridge in Rang Rang. After this 3 km of grade 4-5 all running through but some very long sections. As the volume had increased due to tributaries adding their flow, the frequency and size of large holes and big wave trains with pour-overs increased.

A landslide saw us portaging past a class 6 horror story. More class 4 brought us to Dikchu. Smiling Chris was pleased with his decision. The rest of us were smiling after rising to the 25 km challenge provided by the river.

27th December

From Dikchu, a solid class 4 began the day, we inspected from the road and all decided it would go. 'Good morning' it was named. We loved this section. It consisted of mainly grade 3 big water rapids with 100 m pools between. After a short while, the river left the road as we descended an altitude of 250m during the day. Continuous classes 3 and 4 with calmer class 2 brought splendid variety. Lunch was spent by a lovely, ever-so-friendly play wave, just enough to drag the front end down, thus inducing the kayak to go vertical. This occurred so slowly, unlike so many others where a violent jerk ends the rise. Once vertical there was enough time to spin out. Yes! What fun, again and again. At one point, we pause at a river-wide hole, which one of our team inspected, '*go right, tight right and you will live*' so went right. Soon after, halfway down a longer steeper bouldery class 4 rapid, we came across an unexpected sight. 'Funeral Rapid 'was so named. A funeral pyre had been set alight, the body atop had been pushed into the flow, it bobbed down the left side as we paddled on the right, surreal! Sten managed to find a big hole just below, as did Chris, both getting flushed through and rolling. Next came 'Just Around the Corner', a long class 4, waves and holes increasing in size as the rapid developed. The bottom ended with a right turn where 75% of the flow hit cliffs at 45° causing enormous unpredictable cushions and upwelling boils for 100 m. We sneaked far-right avoiding the mess. At one point 2 house-size boulders 'Double trouble', formed a very long tongue with a fab play wave beneath. Almost at the end, the river split around rocks and ledges guarded the way. We went right, through another large hole, where, yet again Dave rolled. Another fine day had brought us to the village of Makka.

28th December

The early risers claimed they had seen a hoopoe! Today we were to descend 550 m so we were expecting some more choppy sections. However whilst the volume was still reasonably high the difficulties weren't that bad. Long rolling waves interspersed with calmer sections, proved not so technical; consequently, the team felt more relaxed.

After 2 hours of paddling, we needed to inspect. 200 m long with six munching holes lining both sides of the river. Between these barriers, slightly easier water led to a ledge with an awful mess below. But in the middle, a line just misses the first hole on its left, then move left-right between the rest. It even led to a vague tongue through the ledge. As the river was almost 100 m wide, if it went pear-shaped, you would be on your own in the middle of all that. I found the line without problem, the final ledge easier than expected, However, Richard hit the first teasing hole; I waited anxiously below the ledge, relieved as Richard rolled as he was released from the hole. The river was remote, the road high above, yet despite feeling isolated we made good progress. Dave unexpectedly back looped while running through a hole.

Passing under a bridge with huge waves led to 2 km of fun.

Nice water

Above the first road bridge in Singtam, a rapid we named 'Swirly Whirly' saw Gareth caught out again but he rolled. On the bank, at the end of the day, I stood beside Richard as we looked back upstream. Our conversation captured the day;

'*Where is Dave going?*'

'*He's lucky. How did he get away with that? He's not through yet.*'

'*Can't see him, is he dying?*'

'*No. He's OK now.*'

Chris having fun on one of the Teesta's large rapids!

Soon we came to the Camel so-called due to the two humps: first a massive standing wave, second a cushion on a large midstream boulder, with a 2 m pour-over below. The whole lot is guarded by a ledge with a huge midstream boulder. Far-left past the pour-over seemed feasible. Then take the ledge on the left over the wave then move right. Although tricky it paddled without a problem.

Taming the Camel

The difficulties mellowed until we found another, bigger blob at the end of a long pebbly island, its pillows much bigger, but more friendly. At the Radi Kola confluence, we took the bus to a new riverside camp downstream.

Many local women crushed rounded pebbles by hand to make hardcore for roads. They literally bashed rocks with a short-handled lump hammer.

Apparently, they do that all day, every day. I suppose that's one way to earn a wage. Amazingly the few men that hung around, seemed only to be supervising, mostly by chastising the ladies when they stopped bashing with their lump hammers. Occasionally, the men loaded full bags onto a truck and drove away.

Our last day on the Teesta was a repeat of the first two days of paddling, which we strung together. Having driven back upstream to just above the previous day's egress. we rode the Camel again. Richard went big and took the camel direct, ledge, wave and pour-over, straight down the middle, he had very impressive air time into FWD below, after a short stall, then flushed through.

Not another pebble!

We were rather looking forward to playing on our final section, but in the 12 days since we had been there, the river flowed 20 cm lower. The winter cold of the Himalayas had frozen the supply of water somewhat. But still, enough for us to enjoy, without the wonder and stress associated with 'what is around the next corner.'

As we arrived back at camp late that afternoon, the menfolk were still observing the old ladies still crushing rocks.

At breakfast, we noticed some fluttering at the far end of our shingle beach. A closer investigation identified a flock of the hoopoes. Our morning departure for the journey south brought so much laughter as the Teesta and the hoopoes waved us goodbye.

This was the end of the journey – the end of exploring since we first saw a hoopoe in France many years before.

It was the end in more ways than one.

Somewhere Different
Upper Hinterrhine, Switzerland
Dave Hansen, Richard Evans

We enjoyed the challenge of finding new river sections that were not on the usual alpine tours. In the headwaters of the Rhine, the Vorderrhine gorge flows at grade 3 through a deep canyon. Not far away, the other main Rhine feeder a was little gem, the Hinterrhine is full of steep slides and boulders.

Richard Evans, Upper Hinterrhine

A Call from the North

Blackwater, Garve Scotland (March 1992)

Chris Walker-Blackwater

An article in Canoeist magazine caught my eye. Bob Miles from RAF Lossiemouth was looking for some paddlers to join his local guys, to do what he thought would be a first descent of the Blackwater gorge at Garve. I had never heard of it, so I gave him a call. A few weeks later, after a late Friday night drive, we found ourselves in Dallas near Elgin. The following morning, we headed off towards Ullapool and the Blackwater. Fortunately, it was flowing, enough to paddle without a scrape. (We subsequently found out this is rarely the case due to the hydro scheme upstream.) Looking upstream from the road bridge, the first fall seemed a little awkward. Still, we had come this far.

The blackwater is a bedrock river composed of metamorphic psammite rock, quite pointy but smoothed by erosion. Reefs and ridges run downstream parallel to the bank, thus funnelling the flow into narrow channels. Fortunately, the whole section is only 600 m, along with a good track beside it. After a short inspection walk to spy on the issues, we were good to go.

The water had a peaty brown tinge and bright sunshine made the entry falls a lovely 2 m photogenic drop. The second fall under the bridge was higher with an undercut cliff.

Half a dozen lovely but tricky rapids followed, the final drop. 2.5 m into a still pool below another bridge. All went well and only smiles remained.

Final drop

A Long Weekend
Elphin Traverse (March 1993)

The following year, we again visited Bob and his team. Setting off after work, we arrived near Elgin at about 11:00 p.m. Jokingly, we enquired of Bob 'W*here are we off to this* year?' '*An early start I am* afraid,' he replied. We passed Ullapool at about 9:00 a.m. arriving at the head of Cam Loch 30 minutes later. Soon we were off on the journey across nowhere. The flat River Ledmore led us to Cam Loch. The short Abhainn Mhor narrows brought us to the tempting falls of Ea Dubh Uidh a Gulaigeil. The last drop was some 9 m with dubious boils and undercut cliffs on the left, so we portaged.

Drawn on by the lure of the unknown, we progressed across 6 km of Loch Veyatie.

Suilven

220

2 km of narrows underneath the uniquely shaped Suilven, then another 3 km of Fionn Loch brought us to the start of the river Kirkaig.

Class 1 led to 2 then 3 and maybe 4. With every stroke, the tension grew, as we knew somewhere not far ahead were the Falls of Kirkaig, not to be paddled. It could have been an arduous portage. However, Bob had arranged for the RAF Mountain rescue team to do a team exercise. They were there well before us and setting up a series of aerial ropeways. All we had to do was clip the kayak bow and stern on with carabiners, before sending them on their way. Allowing just a short walk down for us. Below the falls the river is rockier and more technical up to grade 4. We had one capsize when Nick lost his paddle. The problems were never too bad, so we managed to read and run until the difficulties eased and we found ourselves on the sea, next to a pristine sandy beach. Our lift back to Elgin was 200 m away. It was a grand day out and likely to have been the first descent of the Kirkaig, all thanks to Bob.

Start of the Kirkaig with Suilven behind

Defeated by the Klamm

Cannobino, Italy, The One that Defeated Us
(June 1995)

John Hough, Richard Evans, Paul McClintock,
Steve Lawrence, Nick Mortimer

Having visited the usual European haunts, we decided to visit Switzerland and Northern Italy. Our river selection was guided by trying to glean information from the DKV (German guidebook). I had perused the guidebooks, deciding the Tessin (Ticino) region seemed like there were adventures to be had. We were partway through our trip at the end of May; having paddled the classic grade 3(4) Vorderrhine gorge, with 300 m cliffs to gasp at. The Albula gorge 3-4 at 80 cumecs had started with the hardest rapid, pleasurable run. The same afternoon, we took in the Moesa, a more open, boulder-filled river, full of challenges at grade 4. The Calancasca attracted the next morning with a mixture of falls, boulder rapids and some short gorges. After a drive south to find the Bavarna, which was a smaller steeper river in a high mountain setting. We inadvertently chased a cormorant under a bridge at the egress. It then proceeded to swim, down the grade 6 section which we had hastily scrambled out to avoid. Maybe it was hungry.

After lunch came the middle section of the Versacca. This is a larger volume river steeper with open, large bouldery sections, intermixed with bedrock falls. Partway down, we were forced to portage, when some guys frantically waved at us from the mid-river. It turns out they were the local mountain rescue team, recovering the body and kayak of a German paddler who, the day before, had paid the ultimate price for a midstream error, which resulted in him becoming pinned under a large boulder. Only the last metre of his boat was visible. It was clearly going to take them a long time. Of course, such an incident makes you stop and think, the question, '*Is it worth it?*' It forces a conscious reset and focus. We proceeded humbly, less chatty than usual, and with more caution.

The Cannobino became our next objective.

The information on the relevant page was scanty at best. And none of our team read or spoke German. Today's literal translation:

'*The Cannobino leads in for a visit question coming section through a wildly romantic, pretty, completely inaccessible gorge. After entering, they will hardly be left. A drive polite therefore only be carried out when the water level is optimal.*

Access: At NW (normal water) (July and August) One is a cheap flow rate of about 3 cumecs. Which please looks quite poor. The maximum for loading drivability would be 5 cumin. Gradient 25 m/km.

Water: very clean

Route: Road 11 at Socraggio (first left upstream – small bowl at the church of St Anna, 4 km)

Difficulties: Comparable to the Kaiserklamm Gorge, Branderburger Ache. Close blocking with falls up to 2.5 m high. Risk of jamming tree closures possible at NW. One siphon. White water 4, 2 passages of 5, 2 passages of X. Possible at NW first visit. If the water level is higher sections in the upper Cannobino, but no further details.'

We couldn't understand too much of this. At the time we had no knowledge of the Kaiserklamm. Stood on the bridge at Lunecco the water level did look like 'a cheap flow rate'. Which we deemed just enough. Seven of us plopped over the 3 m drop just 15 m from the put-in. In a vertical-sided section, small slides brought us to a blind corner. No one fancied being probe, and despite an easy get out, there was no way to see what lay below. We decided to portage. The way in was an abseil back in, we declined. Instead, we decided to drive downstream to the bridge at Socraggio. Repeating the same conversations we just had an hour earlier. There was indecision we should get on.

What if we encounter something similar? Time for 'thumbs' At a count of three we all showed thumbs up or thumbs down. Four up, three down. So, Richard Evans, John Hough, Paul McClintock and I re-entered the 'inescapable gorge' which was mostly 5–8 m wide, vertical-sided. I had such lovely paddling slides and falls, interspersed with flat but flowing water. All went well. A few kilometres along we passed under a road bridge, some 80 m above. A steep stream gully entered just upstream of the bridge, not the sort of thing you would normally choose to egress up, but it triggered a thought. We should keep an eye out for similar places. In this vertical-sided klamm, meandering turns led to a faint roar ahead, and with each bend, it grew louder. With each stroke, the tension grew, just what might we find? It was a stream tumbling into the gorge from above. Phew! A fine place for a shower. Three more class 4 drops, between protruding boulders brought to a halt.

Stood on the right bank we could see a 1 m drop lead across a pool to a 1.75 m drop, after which a 50 m long tricky, slab rapid led into a 6m width of vertical darkness. Hmmm! The left side fall over a boulder looked worse. Choices! We almost decided to retreat to that last horrendous, egress. It would also mean scrambling up the boulders lining the falls that we had just passed, but possible. However, John said he would have a look. Plan A was for him to descend the first drop, then paddle to the left edge of the next drop to see if he could get an eye into the darkness. If needed we could help him back by using throw lines to pull him and his kayak across the intervening pool.

John slid down the first drop but still couldn't see. However, he thought that if he took the next 1.75 m drop, he would get a view and still be able to climb back up if necessary. So with some apprehension, we agreed. Then Scrimblies struck. John slid over the top of the fall, only to be stopped by a 10 cm thick log, wedged underwater, out of sight of us all. After a struggle, John managed to get his arms over the log, but in the process, his paddles went off on their own journey. MOT, he was pinned. Before we could react, only a few seconds later, somehow, the log snaps, releasing paddle-less John down the drop, just out of our sight.

He did half a hand roll, it was enough to find his paddle, which he uses to roll up. Safe? Well no! In the commotion, the flow has pushed John past his point of no return, he has no possible retreat. He paddled to the left bank and managed to scramble out onto bedrock. He shouted, indicating his toe has been cut, by his footrest, through his neoprene boot. We were looking for adventure but now had a situation. At the bottom of a vertical-sided, 80 m deep gorge, John was stuck below, injured. He looked into the darkness downstream and was indecisive. We can't hear him due to the noise of the rapids and the enclosed walls echoing the sound, but he does signal it was a no-go. Plan A, we could retreat and try to escape up that gully thus leaving John alone. After a short chat, Paul, Richard and I hatched a plan B; someone should join John.

We agreed to three options, each of which we assigned a visual signal. A vertical paddle held still ~ all wait for rescue; a vertical paddle waved side to side ~ we all paddle on; a horizontal paddle held above the head ~ you go back and try to escape up that gully and get help. So I volunteered to join John, while Richard and Paul waited.

Since John had cleared the hidden log debris, I slid over the two drops without incident and joined John on the left bank. By the time I reached him, John had applied a dressing to his toe and was painfully squeezing it back into his paddling boot. I decided that the rapid into the darkness did not look that bad. So we elected to carry on. Since the road was high above us on the river right, rescue might be possible. I held my paddle up high, horizontally and point downstream. After getting the thumbs up from Paul and Richard then and watching them depart upstream, with no idea if progress was even possible. We can't stay here. We decide to try. I made a swift ferry glide to gain the main flow, I kept it straight and ran through 50 m of class 4 boulders, and rode clean tongues to the edge of the narrowing. John follows. We were now alone. The water of the chasm was flat but flowing. With overhanging walls, it was darker, until there was an event horizon. As we drift closer more adrenaline kicks in. Just on the lip, there was a small weakness through the river-wide stopper, and a narrow tongue opens up, and we slid through. A second ledge was less obliging, but with speed, momentum overcomes its resistance.

The chasm was now behind us, but we enter an amphitheatre, the left bank is a flat bedrock, backed by high-sided vertical slabs, overhanging higher up. River right was a series of horizontal ledges, with smooth vertical 12 m high, walls. Seventy metres downstream in the klamm the river disappears over another fall. What is the best option? I scan the right wall. At its base, the water was flat but flowing. Just downstream the lowest ledge only 0.3 m above the river was guarded by a riffle. To escape the first difficulty on the ledge, would almost certainly result in a swim. Maybe losing the kayak and maybe being swept downstream with it. It is too risky. Just upstream the flow was calmer, With John's damaged toe, it's down to me to try. I paddled across the current to the cliff, the ledge 1m above water level. Kayaks are not noted for giving a very stable base; I slipped off my spray deck from the cockpit but didn't feel stable enough to just stand up so I could try to reach the ledge. I called John from the other bank and asked him to try paddling forward onto my kayak, to push it against the cliff. It worked: the flow was slow enough that by aiming just upstream, he could hold me in place. By using the bow of his kayak, I could try and stand up. Stop! I realised that if I got out, my kayak would be alone, not secured, and would float off downstream. We crossed back to the left bank, and I used a sling to tie the tow line around my waist to the bow loop of my kayak. I left my rescue kit with John to avoid any chance of losing it. Back at the base of the cliff I used the front of John's kayak to help as I sat on the back of my cockpit. Then gingerly, slowly, hands resting on a vertical rock, I stood up. My kayak wobbles, I tried to relax. My hands rested on the ledge, then I pulled with my arms rather than pushing with my legs, to avoid the kayak moving away from the wall, I mantle-shelved and stand on the ledge.

I was relieved to be on the ledge John wedged my paddle into the cockpit of my kayak and paddled back across the river. I made my way down the ledge, wondering what I might do with my kayak, the ledge was too sloping and narrow to rest the kayak on. A long shot, in my rescue bag, was my one and only climbing nut, a MOAC no 7, a fairly chunky metal wedge. I moved 6 m along the ledge to its lowest point, by that riffle. There, was the only slot in the whole rock ledge. John brought across my rescue kit, and soon I beamed with delight, it was as if it had been made to fit. The slot was deep enough and exactly the right size for the MOAC. The nut was secured to the ledge, my kayak clipped to the rope on the nut with a carabiner.

Now kayakers don't often carry climbing ropes. My throw line was made from polypropylene water-ski tow rope, but needs must. That was the only choice. With a few slings and carabiners from my rescue kit around my shoulder, I immediately became gripped by the prospect. I had given up rock climbing many years ago as being too scary. I enjoy the risk associated with white water kayaking, but climbing was now out of my remit. Above,10 steps, 10 short cliffs, each with a narrow ledge above, 23 m in all were a possible weakness and a way out. The first three ledges were about 1.3 m each, not so bad. From below I could not see where I was aiming for. From the far bank, John was able to guide me right or left, to where he thought there was weakness. At the 6th ledge 15 m up, I had to reach almost as high as I could. Smooth vertical rock was not going to help the grip of my wet paddling shoes. I found two vague knobs for my fingers and pulled up. Just then my left hand suddenly lost grip. I slipped back down making a controlled fall back onto the ledge that I had just left.

With my heart now racing, I really didn't want to try again, but there was no choice, A little voice in my head came to the fore, 'Commit – be positive'. So I tried again, regaining the finger holds and pushing up more aggressively with my feet. Again I mantle-shelved onto the ledge above. The last three steps were comparatively easy, so it was with some glee when I reached flat woodland above and secured the line to a large oak tree. I used a sling to make myself safe in a position where I could see John. Stage 3 sorted.

Using the rope, John was able to tie his kayak on and then stand up, jam his paddle in his cockpit and make the first ledge. He secured his kayak with mine with a tape. I lowered the spare slings, carabiners and my jumar to John who rigged himself a makeshift harness. He pulled a loop from his buoyancy aid. I was amazed to see him able to hang on the polypropylene rope. Then he started to move up, using the jumar, then the prussic. After 8 m he started to tire, His prussic was slipping on the rope and the narrow slings cutting into his legs. After a short rest, he decided to forego the jumar, and transferred to an abseil, then slowly descend using the prussic as a backup. This was in itself was no mean feat. Back on the ledge by the river, he rested. Shouting up and down we reviewed our options. John was safe, for the moment. I suggested that I might head up to the road and try and find help. Thumbs up came from John.

Meanwhile, Paul and Richard had escaped up a gully and been reunited with the non-paddlers. Between them, they had estimated where we might be and were looking for us. I headed up steep wooded slopes and over small crags until… more unbelievable luck! I heard a shout. This was less than 5 minutes after setting off. We were soon united, with big hugs. I led the others to the tree with my line still attached. They had brought a climbing rope and lots of kit, including a harness, which was lowered to John. In a very short time, the 5 of them had pulled up 2 paddles, dragged both kayaks, and John, who leant back on his harness to be propelled up the cliff with some speed. After more hugs and thanks the kit swiftly found its way to the cars. The day had panned out most unexpectedly, but all was well. Even the three thumbs downplaying an integral part of our team. A day for self-reckoning to be sure.

Two years later, we returned. The team was not so keen after the tale of last time. Only Richard and I tried again. This time we were armed with more climbing kit, just in case. The water level was lower; the rapids were less powerful but more tricky. Of course, we knew what to expect. Reaching the darkness that had halted our progress last time. We did not hesitate and ran it on sight. Through the narrow defile. I recognised the escape cliff from the last time. We continued 200 m downstream and stopped just before a 6 m vertical fall. It had a twist at the top. Below narrow and deep, FWD… If you run the fall with this flow you would smash your face on the cliff opposite. Maybe I could capsize to the left as I fall! Never done that before! We eased along a ledge on the left cliff, but the smooth rock failed to reveal anywhere to secure a nut or sling to lower us or the boats from. No other possibilities? We heard thwack, thwack, regularly repeated above, I am certain it is a helicopter. Richard looked puzzled. We had the choice to throw the kayaks down and jump after them, but how would we get back in before the next rapid? Defeated again, disappointed, but best to be philosophical. We had tried. Dragging the kayaks back to that cliff we were faced with plan B. Today, however, it was simpler. The lower flow allowed us to walk across the river to the base of the cliff. Richard fancied the climb. With 2 jumars I followed easily. We soon had secured the kayaks on a rope each, so that we could pull them up quite easily. A surprise of blue flashing lights awaited us at the road. Earlier that day, a tourist had seen us from a bridge high across the klamm and called the rescue services. We were most surprised to find that this was all for us. Soon our team arrived to help us politely retreat from the unwanted commotion.

Lemmings

River Clough, Cumbria

After heavy rainfall Richard Evans and I had decided to paddle one of our favourite rivers, the Upper Clough. It has lots of falls but is rarely paddled. With recent heavy rain, the flow had additional volume. We reckoned the upper section would go. A phone call '*Are you paddling today?*'. Yes, meeting at Sedbergh at 10:00 a.m. to do the Clough from the top. The word was out, and our trip of 2 had become 11, with the Cumbria Coaching team paddlers joining us. It appeared that none of them had paddled the upper section before. On the drive up we purposely omitted to stop at the tricky falls near a road bridge over the river. The river, at a perfect level, soon saw us sliding down slabs and over drops. As we reached the first road bridge, Richard asked if we should tell the others about the next rapid and the fall at the bottom. '*They are all good paddlers I retorted.*' With that, we led off, and they followed. Once you start you don't stop, with 300 m of rapids which get steeper after 200 m. Slides on bedrock with the odd protruding ridge to avoid, a few pressure waves, and the odd hole to skirt or crash through. Then when it gets a bit steeper, everything comes at you faster. You suddenly realise there is a fall at the bottom, but you can't tell how high it is. Here you get thrown right just as you want to go left, fall over the drop half sideways, turn on the lip trying to aim at a right angle to the event horizon, and then boof 2.5 m into the pool below. Some don't make it left, so rush towards the angle, flying sideways into the stopper waiting below. If you edge the kayak and hang there, the stopper fires you along then spits you out.

It is a tricky manoeuvre, even when you know the line and sequence of strokes. Of course, the lemmings did not. Over here, they came in quick succession, three rolled, and two swam. Looks of amazement, excitement, and chat of '*Did we really,*' filled adrenaline-stoked bodies.

So that's how the drop on the Clough acquired its name 'Lemming Falls'.

One Fine Day

Cree, Galloway, (March 2019)

Brian Clough, Sten Sture, Rachel Powell, Martin Powell, Chris Dale

We had taken to spending a couple of weekends each year in Galloway. New rivers to explore. Water levels need to be suitable. Few choose to visit the area despite a great variety of rivers to choose from.

The author falls into…

Going deep

One fine day the water level came just right, and the sun emerged.

Our team was ready for the challenge. Persistence, tenacity and patience are eventually rewarded.

Is it Worth It?

The effort / risk / reward conundrum

To enable a trip to happen, it is necessary to make a big commitment. Time and effort need to be invested in a project with no certainty of success. In the 1980s, pre-internet, research often involved a light bulb moment followed by a stab in the dark. If you were lucky you might know someone who knew someone who might know a little. Magazines were a good source of contact information, followed by a letter or fax or phone call if you were lucky.

Once the principle is established, that a venture might be feasible, bringing together a team becomes the next challenge. Trying to find fellow paddlers with the appropriate skill level, motivation, finances and availability at the right time could be tricky. Then you need to find more information about the proposed river, hotels, transport, flights, first aid, and so the list goes on…

Endless optimism helps.

The effort eventually brings you to the river. All that effort, of just getting there, to knowingly put yourself at risk, as river kayaking is an adventure sport, with unique inherent dangers. However, your own and the team's training, experience, and expertise can minimise, but not remove, the risk. I have discussed the idea of the line of adventure/misadventure. How far do you want to be pushed? Moving that bar higher brings more risk but also major rewards.

The rewards come on many levels: when descending the river there is the continual reward of making progress; finding your way through the three-dimensional mazes; testing your skills which may be close to your limits; the reward of simply being there perhaps where few or no one has been before, enjoying the scenery, geology and wildlife; being able to be adventurous in a unique situation; the reward of taking part in and completing the journey; overcoming the problems both emotional and physical; there is the reward of feeling humble, realising how small and insignificant you really are; and yet, in your mind, you are personally achieving something great.

For me, the greatest reward comes when all these factors are put in the context of exploration. The idea you might just be the first has that indescribable lure and motivates me to do more. During the venture, almost inevitably, there will be times when you got MOT, becoming unsure of the challenge, perhaps simply scared. The reward was only gleaned after you had escaped and survived. Still it is such a great feeling to share the whole thing with good friends. It reaffirms your reliability and trust in each other, strengthens the bond through shared adventure and somehow enhances the sheer pleasure of doing it.

So make the effort efficient, minimise the risks, and then the rewards will flow again and again. Be guided by the hoopoe, avoid the Scrimblies and enjoy.

The author enjoying the BREW, Rio General Costa Rica.

Author, on' 99, with Flake', Fall on Einig River, Scotland 2019

Firsts

The Biggest Challenge

One of the greatest challenges of taking on a new river is, 'Can I do it?'. Even when you have descended a river several times, at different water level there can be a new challenge, or maybe a new tree hazard. Occasionally, rocks move and river beds change.

After exploring their local rivers, most paddlers will start to go further afield, in the same country, or even abroad. The thrill of taking on a new river is quite exciting; questions repeat in your mind. 'What will it be like?' 'Will it be too hard for me?' 'Am I good enough?' We reach for the paddling guidebook. It helps you select something that you think is within the realms of your possibility, within your skill set. A challenge yes, but not too hard. Something small, maybe the description of a rapid or a photo may catch your eye. In the early 1980s, there were few guidebooks. The local guidebook 'Lake District White Water' by Barry Howell, listed 11 rivers. Having paddled most of them I thought there must be more. Whilst taking a bus trip to the North East, looking out of the window as the bus travelled from Sedbergh to Kirkby Stephen, I noticed a valley, on the left. What's down there? I thought. As the bus moved upstream, along the deep river valley, the road became closer to the river. Despite being partly hidden by trees, occasionally, rocky falls could be seen. Later I asked at the local Cumbria paddlers meeting. '*The Rothay?*' no. Most had not heard of the Rawthey. No one seems to know if it had been paddled. Three weeks later, Glen Sutcliffe, his mate and I set off into the unknown. The unknown was enticing but scary. 200 m after setting off his mate decided it was not for him. This was not surprising as he had only paddled a few easy rivers before.

We emerged 2 hours later having managed to paddle all the rapids and drops, up to grade 4. The final gorge was quite intimidating as vertical conglomerate sides would be so hard to climb up if need be. What was around the next corner?

The gorge twisted, with rapids up to grade 3. With some relief, we floated under the Straight bridge at the end of the gorge.

That was fun, challenging, more exciting, and I felt great!

I spent time perusing local OS maps to find new projects. Having listed some possibilities, I recruited various friends to go exploring. It was a little like finding my own 3D mazes to solve. Since we had no previous knowledge to go on, we paddled with care, inspecting when necessary. We worked out the route from the kayak and paddled on sight as much as possible. Running a river without inspection, is much more challenging and so more satisfying, despite more nerve being required. Then in 1988, having accumulated all my newly gleaned information together, I wrote and had published my 'Rivers of Cumbria' paddling guidebook. It details 19 rivers and gives notes on 12 more. At the time, the size of the paddling population was relatively small. I was pleasantly surprised when over 2000 were sold. So much so that a reprint was required adding 5 new rivers in North Lancashire.

As I explored my skill level increased and my confidence grew. So the net of exploration was cast further. As I looked at maps of the Pennines and even the north of Scotland I noticed various rivers next to a main road, the Tirry and Vagastie and Loanan all caught my eye. All of which I finally managed to descend 30 years later in 2016 and 2018, respectively. Such a long time. A 30 year wait to be sure, but so satisfying to successfully complete the project.

Vagastie Falls

Most people I paddled with had visited Briancon in France or Landeck in Austria, but I also looked for other adventures in different locations. Eventually, the lure of new rivers first brought me to the Maha Khali in Nepal and The Rangit, Lachung Chu and Teesta in Sikkim, as you previously read about. It does not really matter who did the first descent. But the idea that you have been where no one else has ventured and contributed to the information pool so that others follow whilst getting to enjoy the river's challenge, is somewhat satisfying. The Vagastie had been paddled by the guys from the local canoe club, but there was only one photo and no description. So we had to find out for ourselves. It is a minor classic if you catch it right. So go explore if you like continuous ... and a few more exciting falls.

Maybe find out for yourself, you will love it. Just portage the steep narrow slide, into a recirculating slot, not far after the second blue fence.

Likely first descents, unless you know better!

Rawthey, Cumbria, May 1982

Lowther, Cumbria, 1984

Sligaghan, Skye, July 1985

Skelwith Force, Brathay, Cumbria, September 1985

Lochy nr Tyndrum, December 1985

Hyndburn, North Lancs, November 1986

Wenning, North Lancs, December 1986

Greta, Ingleton North Lancs, May 1986

Tarennig, Nr the source of Wye, Powys Mid Wales, 1 January 1987

Borrow Beck, Cumbria, January 1987

Roeburn, North Lancs, September 1987

Upper Sprint, above Sadgill farm Cumbria, December 1987

Hafren, Upper Severn Nr Llanidloes Powys, December 1987

Dulas, Nr Llanidloes Powys, December 1987

Allt Chaorainn, Etive, May 1988

Kelthey, Burn Scotland, November 1988

Gloy, Scotland, November 1988

Swindale Beck, Brough, December 1989

Wasdale Beck Cumbria, February 1989

Dee, Dentdale, May 1989

Haukrusti falls, river Lora Norway, August 1989

Upper Kent (from Kentmere Tarn), March 1990

Artle Beck, North Lancs, September 1990

Sleightholme Beck, Tan Hill, Pennines, October 1991

Kiachnish, Fort William, October 1991

Blackwater, Garve Scotland, March 1992

Maha Khali, Nepal, December 1992

Kirkaig, Scotland, March 1993

Rangit, Sikkim, December 1993

Lachung Chu, Sikkim, December 1993

Teesta, Sikkim, December 1993

Deuch Galloway, October 2006

Carron, (Wester Ross), 1 January 2004

Upper Tirry, Scotland, 2016

Cross Water of Luce, Galloway, 2017

Loanan, Highlands, 2018

Minis, Romania, May 2019

Yardstone Beck and Upper Greta (Tees), October 2019

Birkdle Beck (Upper Swale tributary), November 2020

Of course, now 2020, the world is a smaller place. We have a more detailed and more extensive combined knowledge of rivers. Guidebooks are available for many countries. Photos abound on the internet. Many new rivers are now filmed, and movie clips are readily available. We all watch in awe as the 'new adventurers' fall over ever bigger falls, descend ever more tricky rapids, and find more complex 3D mazes which extend to a gorge full of FWD, sometimes for days on end. The time spent underwater amongst bubbles is extended by those whose limits almost seem to have no bounds. Crossing ice sheets, days portaging through the jungle just to get to the put-in, and getting dropped off by helicopter seem to be the way they push the limits.

I am happy to have contributed to the collective knowledge of rivers having had so much fun and camaraderie along the way. But, if you look carefully, take your time, consider the skills of your team, and think about the geology and water level, you might find your own first descent where no one has been there before. Just watch out for the Scrimblies!

You never know what is '**Just around the next corner.**'

Trips Abroad

Richard Evans in the Ubaye Gorge, France

May 1986, Austria

Inn-Tosens, Trisanna, Pitzbach Upper, Stallbach, Sanna, Inn Imst, Rosanna, Lech, Elephants teeth, Ammer, Augsburg.

July 1986, France

Guisanne upper, Durance-Rabiuoux, Onde, Gyronde, Guisanne lower, Guil, Gyr, Ubaye-le martinet, Ubaye-La Fresquiere: Isere.

May 1987, Switzerland

Simmer, Saane, Kliene Emme, Muothal, Vorderrhine, Sanna, Augsburg.

July 1987, Yugoslavia/Italy/Austria

Augberg, Wocheiner Save, Unac, Tara 2 days, Moracca, Kortitnica, Soca, 2 days, Gail, Fella, Tagliamento, Boite upper, Boite Lower, Avisio, Noce, Isarco, Aurino, Rienz, Passer, Oetz, Inn-Imst, Trisanna, Bregezer Ache.

March 1988, Central Massif, France

Ardeche-Pont, Ardeche-upper, Arcdcehe-gorge, Tarn-Vernede
Upper Tarn Gorge, Tarn Gorge Lower, Jonte, Lot-Sallelles, Tarnon, Lot gorge, Allier-St Etiene, Loire-Goudet.

July 1988, Turkey

Isel, Coruh, Una.

December 1988, Nepal

Sun Kosi, Trisuli.

March 1989, Central Massif, France

Tarn Gorge, x2 Middle Dourbie, Dourbie Gorge, Ubaye Gorge, Dora Riparia.

July 1989, Norway

Jostedelva, Bovra, Sjoa, Sjoa Canyon, Frya, Jori, Lora, Driva Melem, Driva-Graura Gorge, Grovu.

Seal launch, upper Dourbie

March 1990, Central Massif, France

Upper Tarn gorge x2 Tarn-Vernede, Lignon, Dore, Allier. Duniers, Lot gorge, Loire, Chaperoux.

July 1990, Costa Rica

General, Sarapiqui, Penas Blancas, Toro, Toro Amarillo, Sucio, Pacuare, Reventaron, Grande di Orosi.

December 1990, Chile

Maipo, Claro 7 teacup, Bio Bio, Pucon, Fuy.

March 1991, Pyrenees France

Petite Nive, Nive de Valcarlos, Gallego, Gave d'Ossau, Ouzo, Noguera Palleresa, Ger, Ariege, Aude.

July 1991, Austria

Loisach, Trisanna, Rosanna, Melach, Inn-Ardez gorge, Inn-Brail gorge, Sesia, Mollia, Diveria, Rhone, Grand Eyvia, Dona de la Thuile.

April 1992, Corsica

Asco, Upper Golo, Travo, Taravo, Liamone lower, Liamone upper, Vecchio.

Nick Mortimer on the Rio Gallego, Spain

August 1992, Tessin Switzerland

Glenner, Reuss-Erstfeld, Reuss-upper, Albula, Upper Hinterhine, Landquart, Inn-Giarsun-Ardez, Oetz main run, Ritzbach middle, Lech Gorge, Rissbach.

May 1993, Maritime Alps/French Alps

Claree, Onde, Bouchet, Guil-Queyeras, Reallon, Ubayette, Ubaye, Bachelard, Verdon, Var.

December 1993, Sikkim

Rangit, Lachung Chu, Teesta.

March 1994
Allier, Truyere.

May 1995
Vorderrhine, Albula, Moesa, Calancasca, Bavarna, Cannabino, Toce, Diveria.

March 1997, Corsica
Vecchio, Taravo, Rizzanese, Liamone, Var, Verdon.

July 1996, Italy/Austria
Kander Reichenbach, Engslinge, Kiene, Weisse Lutschen, Verscacha lower, Cannobino, Noice, Gaderbach, Boite, Ahrnbach, Ruetzbach, Pitzbach middle, Inn-Imst, Melach, Inn-Fleiss.

March 19, Central Massif, France
Allier, Chaperoux, Mimente, Upper Tarn gorge.

August 2000, BC Canada
Babine, Skeena, Bulkey, Stuart (OC).

July 2001, Quebec Canada
Ashuapmushuan (OC).

July 2005, BC Canada
Dease (OC), Upper Stikine (OC).

July 2010, Manitoba, Canada
Bloodvein (OC).

July 2012, Ontario, Canada
Katawagami (OC).

July 2013 Quebec, Canada
Pontax (OC).

August 2014, Finland
Ivalojoki (OC), Kiiminkijoki (OC).

July 2015, Quebec, Canada
Mistassibi (OC).

August 2017, Sweden
Lanio, Piipionjoki, Torne, Tarendo.

June 2018, USA
Middle Salmon, Main Salmon.

May 2019, Romania
Lapus, Rebra, Turku, Baska, Bazou nehoiu, Mare Baska, Boya, Jiu, Riul Mare, Cerna, Minis.

August 2019, Mongolia
Khovd (OC).

November 2019, Argentina
Manso.

July 2022, Finland
Poyrisjoki, (OC) Ounasjoki (OC).

(OC) = open canoe trip

Glossary

Aero – When completely submerged at the bottom of a fall, the feeling of bubbles all around you – like being inside a chocolate aero bar.

Bivi – To sleep out under the stars without a tent.

Boil – An upwelling of water from deep, that falls in all directions.

Boof – Keep the kayak level when descending a fall, to prevent the kayak from going too deep.

Brace – To lean on a breaking wave with a paddle, to gain support and prevent capsizing.

Break out – Manoeuvring a kayak from flowing water into an eddy.

Break in – Manoeuvring a kayak from an eddy into flowing water.

Bubbleosity – When the percentage of bubbles at the bottom of a fall is so high, you sink into it, rather than float on top.

Capsize – When a kayak becomes inverted.

Canogining – Sliding down snow in a kayak.

Cfs – American measure of river flow, cubic feet per second.

Cumec – A measure of river flow, cubic metres per second.

Cushion – When water flows against a cliff or obstruction a cushion forms on the upstream side of the obstacle.

Eddy – The slack water behind a boulder or at the river's edge.

Edge – To lean the kayak to counteract the force of the river flow.

Ender – When the back or front of the kayak goes vertical. Sometimes caused by a stopper.

Event horizon – A level of flat smooth water, before a fall, that you cannot see over until you are on the edge.

Fall – A rapid with a more vertical nature.

Gradient – The steepness of a river section, ‰, given in metres per kilometre.

Gorge – A section of a river where both banks are bound by vertical rocks or cliffs, they can be huge or small.

Haystack – An exploding wave formed where too much water flows through a narrow gap.

Jumar – A device used to climb a vertical rope or to give tension to a rope.

Klamm – A narrow gorge, maybe only a few metres wide, with high cliffs.

Ledge – A horizontal bedrock feature that has a fall below.

Nut – A piece of metal placed in a crack to which a rope can be secured.

Pinned – When a kayak is trapped by a river bed feature, usually boulders.

Pop-out – When a kayak is vertical after being released from a hole or whirlpool. Also called an ender.

Pool – Flat still section of the river.

Pour-over – Waterfalls over a large boulder causing a hole to form below.

Probe – The first person down a rapid or fall.

Prussic – A knot used to do the same function as a jumar.

Rapid – A disturbance in the smooth flow, caused by a change in gradient and formed by features on the river bed.

Riffle – A clean green wave formed as deepwater flows over a bedrock ledge or line of rocks. Can be good to surf on.

Roll – A paddle stroke used to right an inverted kayak.

Scrimbly – A mischievous mythological river monster.

Slab – A smooth inclined bedrock feature, usually with a stopper or standing wave at the base.

Squiggly – An inexperienced Scrimbly.

Siphon – Where water flows and disappears through a narrow underwater slit or gap between boulders.

Standing wave – A wave that stays in the same place relative to the river bed. May be smooth or have a breaking top.

Stopper/hole – A wave where the top falls back upstream into the bottom of the wave. The water recirculates, and when big enough, can stop or trap a kayak or kayaker.

Undercut – Where a cliff or boulder is angled low over the river.